Scar Tissue

Scar Tissue

A Tale of American Armor

Shannon Frison

Scar Tissue / Shannon Frison

ISBN: 979-8-9988072-2-0

Library of Congress Control Number: 2025913520

Book cover design by Global.Dezine

The Author's Journey Publishing Co.

Journey Imprint

Old Hickory, TN

Dedication

This book is dedicated to my grandmomma and granddaddy, the late Mrs. Jessie Mae Frison and Mr. E.L. Frison. What a progeny you have left, and we are giants because of you. I am forever humbled by the lives you led. Thank you for our clan; I know you are proud of us.

Contents

Acknowledgements

I have so many to thank for this book coming to life. In addition to every person who has read it, I dearly thank:

My wife, Lovita Page, for cracking the whip when I slacked up on writing and always pushing me to be the best version of Shannon Frison I can be;

My mother, for being the consummate guide through life that you are to me. If only I can remain on the planet with the grace that you show everyday, I will consider myself lucky and in God's favor;

My sister Jaime for her love, patience, wisdom and always being Team Shannon no matter what;

My aunts Brenda, Linda, Emma, Mary, Tina, and Ruby; and my uncles Jessie, Tommy, Charlie, Alex, and William for the oral history you shared with me to make sure I got it right about the Frison family and grandmomma and granddaddy;

My friend and college roommate Paitra for reading the very first morass of stories and giving me the first guidance as to how to bring this piece to life and make it readable;

All of my roommates, Shannon, Chris, and Paitra for your lifelong friendship and love, and for always supporting my crazy endeavors;

My aunt Mary for always being an example to me, always backing me in the hardest of times, and for reading and reviewing this work;

Every reader and reviewer who shared my story and talked about it;

My publisher and editor, Elona Washington, and The Author's Journey for believing in me from day one. And for literally making this book a reality. Your guidance and expertise is without match;

IngramSpark for bringing my words to paper and to the world; and

My daughter, Malakhai, for making me smile every day that I am with her.

Foreword

It is both daunting and humbling to write a foreword for my dear friend and esteemed colleague, Shannon Frison. She has lived multiple lives and lived each well. It wasn't always (ever?) easy, but with military precision and intense commitment, she persevered. And with that perseverance came fruits that continue to nourish those within her ambit. Having known Judge Frison for a couple decades now, I have witnessed firsthand the unwavering dedication, resilience, and brilliance she brings to the field of law. Her journey, intricately woven with personal and professional trials, is a testament to her strength of character and her relentless pursuit of justice.

Judge Frison painstakingly unveils not only her experiences as a lawyer but also the profound impact of her background and identity on her practice. The prologue captures a pivotal moment in her career—a court-martial that challenged not just her legal acumen but also her resolve in the face of racial bias. This narrative, alarmingly familiar to Black professionals, reveals the complexities of navigating a system that often presumes the incompetence of those who do not fit the traditional mold.

As a former judge, Frison has seen the law from both sides of the bench. Her insights into the intricacies of the military justice system and the profound challenges faced by her clients reflect her deep understanding of the human condition. She has fought valiantly for those who often lack a voice, standing firm against the biases that seek to undermine their dignity and humanity. Justice has served as her consistent lodestar throughout her life and career.

Her story is not just one of legal battles; it is also a reflection of her commitment to equity and her belief in the transformative power of advocacy. By and through her narrative, she invites us to consider the scars we all carry—those visible and invisible— and how they shape our lives and careers. In her powerful examination of identity, resilience, and justice, Judge Frison encourages us to confront our many priors and work for a more inclusive future.

The operative word in the previous system is "work." Judge Frison embodies the view that justice is not some airy concept without practical application. Through her stories, she knows that advocates must make justice happen. Justice will not simply materialize from whole cloth. People— everyday, ordinary, concrete people—make justice happen by action and deed. Judge Frison makes justice happen every day.

This is not a book packed with staid legal discourse; rather, it is a call to action. The book is not simply theory; it is hortatory. It reminds us that our struggles are interconnected and that the pursuit of justice is a shared journey. She invites the reader to join her on this magnificent journey.

Judge Frison's narratives will resonate across age, race, and culture. The book's message ignites a passion for justice, a value that is core to Judge Frison's being.

Ronald S. Sullivan Jr.

Jess M. Climenko Clinical Professor of Law, Harvard Law School, Cambridge, MA, September 2025

Preface

I knew she would be kicked out of the Navy with a dishonorable discharge. She knew that too. But my goal was to represent her at the court-martial, save her life, and keep her out of the brig. What I didn't know was that I would face another run-in with racial bias. As a Black woman living in America and graduating from Harvard University, it was something I was already all too familiar with. Still, I didn't expect to face it while arguing a case in court.

During this time, I was a solo practitioner. As you will read in this book, I was a civilian prosecutor for the Commonwealth of Massachusetts. I also served as a judge advocate in the Marine Corps, and prior to that, I worked for a law firm in Boston doing litigation. So I had been several years removed from military life when this case came across my desk.

I thought I knew everything about that life. After all, I had been on active duty and held the rank of Major in the Marine Corps, a mid-level officer responsible for managing operations and people. Many civilians don't realize that officers and enlisted members operate on entirely different rank structures. Technically, the lowest officer outranks the most senior enlisted Marine, but anyone who's seen a Sergeant Major in action knows respect is not about rank alone.

Still, for all my experience, nothing prepared me for what I learned while defending this sailor: how deeply gang activity had infiltrated even the military. Even the disciplined ranks of the Marine Corps were not immune.

My client was a Black woman who held the title of Master Chief Petty Officer of the Navy, the highest-ranking non-commissioned officer in the branch. That is a serious achievement. The position serves as the voice for all enlisted sailors and advises top Navy leadership on their needs, challenges, and morale. And she was married to a Marine. His pregnant mistress was also a Marine. The man she allegedly persuaded to murder the mistress was a Marine as well. All of them were stationed in Okinawa, Japan.

The government accused my client of plotting the mistress's murder with members of the Crips, a street gang she and her husband counted as friends. Prosecutors claimed she orchestrated a "virtual hit" through phone and email, directing gang members in North Carolina to carry out the shooting. They argued the conspiracy stretched from Okinawa to Iraq and North Carolina, with coordination happening across continents. The alleged plot unraveled only because the would-be shooters backed out when they saw the intended victim had a child with her. No blood was shed, but the Navy moved forward with plans to prosecute her for the failed assassination attempt.

So my client was formally charged with conspiracy to murder in addition to several other offenses. As an independent lawyer, I managed every aspect of that general court-martial myself. The military trial system has rules that may be unfamiliar to civilians, including civilian lawyers. One of them is that your presence is always required, so I flew to Japan several times to represent her.

I prepared my client for testimony and sentencing, drafted questions for each witness, including her husband, NCIS officers, and investigators, wrote and argued motions to reduce or weaken the charges, conducted voir dire, challenged members who should not sit on the panel, and delivered opening and closing arguments. At the same time, I managed her expectations about the possible outcome.

In a case this serious, a typical defense would involve an entire team of four to six professionals, often including multiple lawyers, paralegals, investigators, and expert witnesses. I shouldered all of those responsibilities on my own while coping with jet lag, adjusting to Japanese culture and daily life for weeks at a time, and working in the sweltering Okinawa heat and humidity. Okinawa is tropically hot, the kind of heat that clings to you, soaks your clothes, and forces your body to adjust. Traveling back and forth to defend someone who looked like me, someone facing the most serious trouble of her life, was both terrifying and invigorating. It became quite the education for a hungry defense lawyer.

When I first met my client, I saw a Black woman close to my age who had been emotionally abused, cheated on, humiliated, and harassed by a pregnant mistress. And she was finally trying to gain control of her life. But the members of the court-martial wove a story of infidelity and revenge, linking her romantically to a Crips gang member through a string of emails. To say the least, it was a very difficult case to defend.

The commanding officer selects the jury in a court-martial, which includes service members at and above the accused's rank. For my client's trial, they were largely, if not all, men. And they were predominantly, if not exclusively, Caucasian. The jurors ranged in rank from senior enlisted to full-bird colonel. The colonel was considered the senior member and, like all things military, ran the jury with added responsibility for guiding the group and ensuring procedures are followed.

The trial took place at the Joint Law Center on Camp Foster in Okinawa, Japan. The building was stark. The atmosphere was impersonal, and the courtroom felt cold and looming, much like the legal process itself. I had been there before, but never in this capacity. I was nervous but excited, too. My client was seated next to me. She looked scared but strong. At the table next to us was the prosecutor, referred to as a "trial counsel" in military terminology. I knew him from my years on active duty as a judge advocate. In fact, I had served alongside him on the very military base where the trial took place. All the jury members sat in a box to our left. My defense and my client were well-prepared, but like most trials, you never know what might happen.

From the elevated bench directly in front of us, the military judge presided over the courtroom. I also knew him from my time prosecuting in the Corps, specifically in Okinawa. This would be my first time appearing in front of him as a civilian attorney representing a servicemember. Marines and sailors have the option of hiring their own privately retained counsel for criminal matters. That day, it was me. There's a well-known saying among lawyers: a good lawyer knows the law. A great lawyer knows the judge. Despite everything that was stacked against her, my client was in good hands.

As a lawyer, you brace yourself for the twists and turns that come with a trial, but nothing prepares you for being put on trial yourself. The senior member of the jury asked the judge, "I'd like to know if the tattoos her lawyer has are gang-related." I couldn't believe he asked that about me. The lawyer who traveled 7,500 miles to defend this servicemember. The lawyer who dedicated more than a year of work preparing for trial. Above all else, the lawyer who was also a United States Marine. How dare he mistake me for a gang member, someone who did not go to Harvard, did not excel, and did not follow the straight and righteous path to success in this country. How dare he not even recognize that he was talking to a Marine officer just two ranks below himself. He saw me—Black. He saw my client—Black. He saw her husband—Black. He saw the alleged victim—Black. He saw the alleged co-conspiring gang members—Black. And that was all.

This was also my first experience with tattoo bias, and to put it mildly, I was mortified. Horrified. He could barely see the tip of a tattoo on my clavicle. Seriously? At the time, I didn't have nearly as many tattoos as I do now, and certainly not enough for anyone to be commenting on in a courtroom. Quite frankly, his accusation was ridiculous. The combination of gang violence, Black people, and tattoos created its own special brew of racism, stereotypes, and prejudices. This meant that defending the trial would be even more difficult.

Despite the attack on my character, I maintained my composure. I was there to work. I was there to save this other stellar Black woman from charges, from military prison, from racism, from chauvinism, from everything that I had wanted someone to save me from.

Luckily, the military judge saw the moment for what it was. Without answering the senior member's question about my tattoos, the judge quickly dismissed him from the jury. Upon the jurors' release for the day, only the judge, prosecutor, and I remained. When we brought up that ridiculous question from the colonel, we all exploded into raucous, belly-rolling, knee-slapping laughter. But beneath my laughter was a still and stagnant sadness. Perhaps instead of laughing, we should have been talking about how, no matter what I do, I would face racism where they wouldn't. That I would always have an extra burden that they, as white men, would never have. Despite my achievements and skills in my craft, I still felt like a suspicious Black person at the end of the day.

Even with his removal, it was a long and dramatic trial. The evidence had been stacked against her. To add fuel to the fire, her husband had recently been convicted in a Japanese court for a near-deadly assault on a Japanese national. He was serving an eight-year prison sentence. The investigation also implicated other service members allegedly affiliated with the Crips. A series of sultry, revealing emails to the gang member she was accused of contracting painted my client as an angry, vengeful, and scorned wife who had allegedly been romantically involved with the Marine she asked to kill the mistress. It was a complicated set of relationships amongst these young service members. But my only interest in the whole affair was getting my client out of it. In the end, I did just that. She and I made it out of Okinawa intact but not untouched.

Despite the mountain of evidence against her, none of it proved she was guilty of conspiracy. As a result, she was acquitted of most charges but convicted of a minor offense and dishonorably discharged from the Navy. As awful as that sounds, it was a true victory. She would not go to the Brig. She would remain free.

As for me, my pride was hurt, eyes opened, and armor hardened. I left the courtroom with a mission. I was determined not to let racism color my defense of anyone charged with crimes. I wanted to turn bias on its head through my work and my advocacy.

As I stepped outside the Joint Law Center with my client, the heat swallowed us whole. But that day, the heat wasn't just in the air. The heat that I felt rising within me originated in the air-conditioned courtroom, intensified by the sting of bias and the quiet resolve that settled in my chest as I walked to my car. My client and her sister, who was also a sailor, smiled and thanked me before I climbed into my rental car.

We had no visible scars, no visible bruises, no blood, no broken bones; but still, we left wounded. The kind of wounds that don't scream. The kind that settle deep under the skin, attach to the muscle, and harden over time. But I left Okinawa with a mission: to defend my clients without letting racism distort the way I fight for them and to expose that bias through the power of the law itself.

Racism, humiliation, and betrayal don't always manifest outwardly. Occasionally, they sit quietly in your body and make a home. My body tells that story. It's marked by tattoos I chose later in life and by scars I never asked for, some of them etched into me before I could even speak. This book is about those marks. The ones I carry in silence. The ones that shaped me. The ones that remind me how even when you do everything "right," you're still not safe. Not in this country.

We were raised to believe in the great American Dream. In our twenties and thirties, we believed in the formula: work hard, follow the rules, get the degrees, buy the house, shake the right hands. We believed acceptance would follow. But by the time we reach our forties and fifties, we realize it was all an exercise in futility. We played by the rules, and still, we were cut. Again and again. Death by a thousand cuts, each one small enough to dismiss but together deep enough to wound. Those cuts become scar tissue, and that scar tissue becomes both your armor and your teacher. A warning, a protection, and a map. A way to move through a world that sees your skin before your soul. A way to survive these United States.

That's why I wrote this book. Because I know I'm not the only one carrying these kinds of scars. Because I have spent a lifetime watching brilliant, dedicated people follow every rule only to be pushed aside, questioned, or erased. I wrote this for the ones who were told they didn't belong even when they were overqualified. I wrote this for those who swallowed their pain just to make it through the day. I wrote this for the professionals who work twice as hard and still get asked if they belong in the room.

I wrote this now because silence no longer serves me. And I hope that in reading this, you feel seen, you feel truth rise up in your story, and you find strength in the marks you have carried too long in silence.

Childhood & College
Scars of Origin

My grandparents' home in Panola County
Mississippi, a Jim Walter house

Me, Sardis, Mississippi cotton field, 2018

Chapter One
May The Road Rise Up to Meet You

Jessie Mae Frison. At the risk of echoing the opening line of *A Tale of Two Cities* by Charles Dickens, I must embrace the contradiction: her funeral was both majestic and devastating. A day of beauty and heartbreak. So many people. So many people. Not just family, but friends, some of whom I, the eldest granddaughter, had never met. Old and young, men and women, working and unemployed, healthy and frail. Each face drew me back to a moment when my grandmother, Jessie Mae Frison, was still alive.

It was June of 2000, not long after I had completed my tour of duty in the Marine Corps. I was at my grandparents' house for my grandmother's funeral, and I woke up with a headache and a nervous stomach to keep it company. Everyone moved about the house, showered, and dressed like any other Sunday, but I sensed they felt the same as I. We were heading to Antioch Baptist Church, our family church, located on the border of Courtland and Pope, Mississippi. It is a small church in a rural area of the poorest state of the U.S. Nothing is next to it, and the only thing across the street from it is the graveyard. The building is old, has only one level, and smells like old Bibles and wooden pews. Yeah, there was air conditioning, but some days it didn't feel like it.

Since I was a child, Antioch maintained a small congregation of faithful attendees, a Black male pastor, a familiar choir, and a warm atmosphere. Every time I stepped into that church, I thought, "This must be how it felt to go to church as a slave in the United States." I imagined our ancestors taking all their swords and shields, all their worries and fears, all the weight of servitude to the altar. Even though they were bound to the fields—this one day, this one hour, they felt free.

The night before, I had sat down on the couch across from my grandfather, and he asked, "How you, Jib?" My grandfather calls me Jib. I don't even know how I got that nickname. But, from my granddaddy, just about everyone got a nickname. So 'Leen, Jack, Poncho, Buck, Snake, Brownskin, Tootsie, Pig, etc. are all nicknames for folks in my family. And don't try not answering to your nickname. Ain't gonna work. When I'd call and tell him it was Shannon on the phone, he'd have no idea it was me. My name is "Jib." His "Jib."

I responded, "I'm alright, I guess."

And he said, "Well, everyday aint gon' be Sunday..." It was his way of saying life won't always be easy or sweet. Some days come with grief, with heartache, with the kind of heaviness that cannot be prayed away. Then Granddaddy went on to talk about how he and Grandmomma knew that they would have to leave each other one day.

"We all gotta do what she did—go on away from here."

I just sat there and nodded in affirmation, knowing that his pain was 55 years greater than my own, wondering how he could be so strong. Then again, 'strong' doesn't even capture the kind of fortitude he passed down to all of us, like the way he used to toss each of us a silver dollar for candy, easy and sure, like it was second nature.

At 11:30 a.m., my grandmother's house held family members who had traveled from Mississippi, Memphis, North Dakota, Chicago, and St. Louis. My grandmother's house is the "home house." The entire Frison family congregated at this house for everything important: Christmas, Thanksgiving, birthdays, anniversaries, reunions, meetings, crises, and fellowship. Just about all of my aunts and uncles have lived in that house and returned to it in times of trouble. It is now my mother's house.

Like many families across the South, ours lived in a Jim Walter home. As a child spending summers in Mississippi, I often heard people point and say, "That's a Jim Walter house," without knowing what it meant. I do now. After World War II, Jim Walter Homes sold affordable shell houses that were often the only path to homeownership for Black families in the South, especially returning Black veterans who were shut out by discriminatory laws and lending practices. These houses came with nothing beyond framed walls. No electricity. No plumbing. No insulation. No heating or air.

My aunt Emma told me she bought her house that way and had to add everything herself. The workmanship was not perfect, and making them livable took a lot of time and money, but for families like my grandfather's, it was a rare chance to set down roots and call something their own.

My grandparent's house is small, old, and in need of repairs, but it remains ours. My mom and at least four of my aunts in Mississippi still live in theirs, all paid off after years of hard, steady work.

That house has held decades of our laughter, our arguments, our prayers, and our grief. It stood with us again on the day we gathered to say goodbye. So many people came that the walls could not hold us all. We filled the yard, crowded onto the porch, and crossed the road to where my grandfather keeps his cows, hogs, chickens, and goats.

Almost everyone was dressed in black. Standing in the yard, I beheld my wonderful and close-knit family. A proud family. I marveled at a cousin, uncle, and niece whom I had not seen in so long. However, each time my heart swelled with joy at the reunion, I felt a knot in my stomach as I remembered the reason for our gathering: Grandmomma has passed away. It was majestic, yes, but it was the worst day of my life.

We eventually arrived at the church, and it smelled just as I remembered, and it gave the same familiar feeling. Sitting on the left were friends, and the pews on the right were reserved for us. At the altar was a white casket, and inside was a woman who had lived 73 years for her God, her husband, and her 12 children. My legs buckled as each pair of us stopped briefly at the casket. Grandmomma wore a white dress and a magnificent white hat. She loved hats. As my sister, Jaime, and I got closer, I grabbed her hand for strength so that I would not fall or double over. She seemed to be sleeping, but I knew better. My stomach did flips and somersaults and danced, and that movement was the only thing that kept my legs from becoming icy cold and frozen.

Finally, Jaime and I stepped up to the casket. It was Jessie Mae Frison, looking good as usual. When I visited her in the hospital a few months prior, she was small, her hands bowed by atrophy, unresponsive, with machines barely keeping her tethered to this side of life. I wanted God to take her then because I knew she was suffering. But today she looked as if she had gotten up, gotten dressed, and headed to a Mother's Day service, an occasion when all of the church mothers and elders wore all white. It was a struggle not to run out of there.

My great uncle gave a touching eulogy, but I faded in and out as my eyes drifted back and forth from my grandmother to my mother to my screaming great aunt. I cannot tell you how long the service lasted. I can only tell you that it was too short. Too short before the mortician closed the casket and made it the last time I would ever see her again. My knees and ankles, shins and toes, weakened as they rolled her out of the church into the tent. The preacher said words that I could not hear as I searched for my mother. I had to find her and hold her. I found her holding my sister close and whispering, "Say goodbye," through her tears as she watched them lower the casket into the ground. My aunt Emma burst into tears as the casket finally disappeared. I watched in awe as the workers covered the grave. I thought, "No, no, I must get her out of there." But I could not.

The ride home was somber, and when we got back to the house, I sat with my grandfather. I wanted to be next to him. Then he said out of nowhere, "Every Sunday I carry her to church and carry her back to the house. Today, we went to church, but I couldn't bring her back..."

The next day, I did not say much to Granddaddy. I would not have been able to speak even if words had come to me. As the eldest, I watched my mother closely, ready to catch her if her knees gave out from grief.

That house, like the land it stands on, has been and always will be a part of me. Looking around at the faces on the porch and in the yard after the funeral, I was reminded of my earliest years here, when I was a country baby on my grandmother's knee.

Chapter Two
From Cotton to Concrete

My mom had me when she was 24 years old, after moving to Chicago as part of the Second Great Migration. In those days, everyone Black in Chicago seemed to have roots in Mississippi. But when I was born, she brought me to the Sip and placed me in the care of my grandparents, where I stayed until I was old enough to attend school.

For my first few years, I spent my days at my granddaddy's heels. I followed him as he hauled wood in the hot sun, hung out in the cornfields, played with farm animals, and rode go-carts, bikes, and anything else with wheels. I loved the smell, taste, and sound of the South.

My grandparents raised me, which meant I was raised by Mississippi sharecroppers.

Sharecropping is an agricultural system from the post-Civil War South where white landowners leased land to farmers (white and Black) in exchange for a share of the crop yield. My grandparents raised 12 children in the 1940s and 50s under the crushing weight of this system. Sharecropping was presented as a step forward from slavery, but in reality, it was a system designed to keep landless farmers trapped in poverty and debt. The majority of sharecroppers were white, yet for Black families it carried the added weight of racism, ensuring they remained poor, landless, and dependent on white landowners.

My mother and aunts told me they moved constantly because my grandfather's ability to keep a roof over their heads depended on the quality of the land he was given, the mood of the white landowner, and the weather. Sometimes it was not even about the land or the crop. One season, my grandfather and family were put out for registering to vote. That was the level of control these landowners had. They could take away your home, your livelihood, and your stability simply because you tried to exercise your rights.

The cruelty of sharecropping has not ended. While it is much less common, white landowners and local officials still use the same principles to keep Black farmers in economic bondage. The same families that have been in charge for generations control access to land, credit, and fair equipment prices. Black farmers are still denied bank loans unless they agree to sell their crops through white-owned gins at unfair prices. Others are promised better land "next season" if they work harder, a promise that is rarely kept. The mechanics have changed just enough to make it look legal, but the purpose is the same: keep us working, keep us poor, and keep us from building wealth we can pass on.

Because of my Southern roots, I know the value of an honest day's work and the unspoken rules of the South. I know how to shell peas and make cha cha, a preserved relish of green tomatoes, cabbage, and peppers. I know how to steer clear of sundown towns and how to keep moving in the face of overwhelming odds. In Mississippi, Black folks have had to thrive against the impossible every single day. I did not yet know it, but those lessons would steady me as a Marine, guide me as a lawyer, and shape me as a judge.

Growing up, I never felt that my situation was bad. I never felt poor or disadvantaged. We had what we needed and could do what we wanted. I didn't notice the Mississippi segregation I was living in. I was surrounded by Black folks, in a mostly Black part of Panola County, wrapped in the love of a big family. For me, there were no scars.

However, my grandparents bore scars from that life. My granddaddy walked with a slight hitch, one leg a little longer than the other from a damaging bout with childhood polio. My grandmother walked with the deliberate pace of a woman who had birthed a total of thirteen children and endured a lifetime of Southern medicine. They also carried the scars of a medical system that never valued Black bodies, from the Tuskegee Experiment to forced hysterectomies to Ms. Henrietta Lacks. For those reasons, they taught us to protect our bodies and heal ourselves with what we had.

When I was old enough for preschool, my mother brought me north to Chicago. Every summer after that, I returned to Mississippi. I have always felt lucky to have spent my life toggling between the city and the country.

In Mississippi, I woke to roosters, fields, and the smell of the earth. In Chicago, I woke to sirens, concrete stairwells, and the sound of kids playing outside. The country gave me open sky, dirt roads, and fields of cotton. The city gave me brick apartments, crowded sidewalks, and the hum of traffic that never stopped.

The South was peaceful and grounding, and I preferred the country. Still, I instinctively knew I would need the opportunities the city offered. Moving between the two shaped me in ways that growing up in only one never could.

Even today while living in the Northeast, I make sure Mississippi stays with me. During the fall of 2022, my cousin, Bernardo, and I picked cotton in Panola County, Mississippi, to use as decoration in my house. When we pulled the stalks out of the ground, not many of the buds had opened. Bernardo said to soak them overnight, then dry them in the sun. I followed his directions, and in a day or two, the rest of the buds opened just like he said they would. Why does my 50-year-old cousin know so much about cotton? For years, he oversaw the entire cotton gin in Pope, Mississippi. I am proud of that and of him. We lead completely different lives in different states, yet I have immense respect for the skills he mastered: welding, cotton gins, horse breaking, and more things I would not know the first thing about. I am proud of him and of my whole family for surviving and thriving, producing, and reproducing in a hostile environment.

Displaying cotton stalks as art in my home serves as a reminder for me and for anyone who walks through my door of our shared legacy of bondage and survival. "King Cotton" was a slogan used before the Civil War by Southern secessionists to claim that cotton made the South so economically powerful that it could thrive independently from the North. They believed that controlling cotton exports would force Britain and France to support the Confederacy militarily because their economies depended on Southern cotton. That theory failed, but cotton's role in the enslavement, servitude, and oppression of Black people in the South is undeniable. Even today, white people own 97 percent of cotton fields and their profits.

During all those years of sharecropping labor, my family remained lower class in Panola County, never gaining lasting stability. The little money they made went to finishing the house and feeding the children. The grand homes in Batesville stood in sharp contrast to ours: mansion against shanty.

No one talks enough about the moment you realize you are part of the neglected class in this country. That realization hits people differently. Some turn to crime, some work harder, some give up entirely. But shame is common to us all.

For me, that feeling became fuel. I refused to be trapped in the lower class in a country that claimed everyone could succeed. I knew I had too much to offer the world. My family encouraged me, even when they did not fully understand my path. In the Frison family, if you were good at something, we pushed you to do it to the fullest. I never let the sight of our houses compared to white mansions make me feel inferior. It simply pushed me to excel. I was physically fit and a natural leader, so the Marine Corps was a good choice for me. I was an avid reader and thinker with a strong sense of justice, so law fit me as well. I may not have known then exactly how I could fight inequities and disparities, but I knew my life's journey would matter to me, my family, and Black people as a whole.

That hunger showed up when I was a little kid in Chicago, where growing up poor meant growing up fast. I was the eldest of two girls, living with our mother in a small apartment on the South Side. I was a tomboy, a reader, a natural athlete, a leader, and a budding scholar. When you are poor, you learn about life sooner. You worry about money sooner. You start working sooner. You learn how to help run the home and care for siblings sooner. There is little time for coddling or the luxury of an untroubled childhood.

That hunger, like most eldest daughters in Black families, turned into overachievement. For me, it began with public speaking at my kindergarten graduation. At the time, I was attending a Catholic school (though I was not Catholic) where discipline was strict and sometimes harsh. It was not unusual to get whacked on the knuckles with a ruler for giving the wrong answer.

One day toward the end of the school year, my teacher called me to her desk. I thought, "What did I do now?" I walked up slowly, bracing myself for punishment. Instead, she handed me a sheet of paper and told me she wanted me (me?) to recite the Pledge of Allegiance at our graduation ceremony. I was filled with pride and took on the assignment eagerly. Nightly in our small South Side apartment, I practiced with my mother. By the time graduation came, she was probably tired of hearing it, but she showed up for my graduation to hear it again. She was proud and encouraged me to do well.

I had it memorized cold. But when I got to the school auditorium, my stomach turned and I became nauseous. I ran to the bathroom and vomited just moments before my performance. I thought, "Oh no, this is going to ruin everything." Fortunately, it did not. My mother helped me clean up, and I marched right out and delivered a flawless Pledge of Allegiance to the audience. Thirty-two years later, I found myself in a similar situation— dressed up, just seconds away from an important speech, and filled with nausea. This time, it was in Suffolk County Superior Court in Boston, just before my closing argument in the biggest murder trial the city had seen in decades.

I spent kindergarten and first grade at that Catholic school, but after my mother married, we moved, and I transferred to Adam Clayton Powell Elementary. The school was new in those days, just opened in the mid-70s, and while it was not city-wide famous, in South Shore it mattered. From 2nd through 8th grade, Powell became my home, a pro-Black, truth-telling, supportive, and nurturing environment.

By the time I finished eighth grade at Adam Clayton Powell Elementary, the path ahead felt open and urgent. High school would test that hunger. I was about to trade red dirt roads and brick stairwells for court filings, train rides, and choices I was too young to recognize as dangerous.

Chapter Three
Growing Pains

I attended high school at Hyde Park Career Academy on the South Side of Chicago. My mother worked at the University of Illinois, which offered a program that covered the summer wages of employees' children working in professional offices. During my freshman year, I qualified through this program and spent my first summer at an all-Black law firm on Chicago's South Side. I worked as a secretary and intern, supporting attorneys Anthony Ferguson, Gregory Miller, Terry Stallings, Eric Graham, Oliver Spurlock, and Robert Willis, who practiced in criminal defense, real estate, entertainment, family, and probate law. The real secretary, Janice, was a middle-aged Black woman who ran the office and taught me everything I know about law offices and professionalism. A Chicago native, she was attractive, confident, grounded, assertive, amiable, and a natural teacher. I absorbed everything she shared with me. The experience was fascinating and formative, and it sparked my passion for the law.

Eventually, the attorneys trusted me to write letters to clients, draft documents, and travel downtown to file pleadings. I would take the "L" train from 95th and State to the courthouse, deliver the pleadings to the clerk's office, and get a stamped receipt. At my age, this was enormous fun because it gave me independence, let me explore downtown stores like Garrett's Popcorn, and instilled in me a strong sense of responsibility and professionalism. When the program ended, the attorneys chose to keep me on and pay my wages themselves for the following summers. Anthony Ferguson would even ask before summer break how much I needed to earn and then make sure I was paid that amount. If only every job afterward had allowed me to name my salary. That experience was my first real foray into the legal world and the spark that convinced me to pursue a career in law.

During this time, I had my first experience with the darker side of human nature. When it happened, I truly thought it was no big deal and my fault. Years later, I would come to understand that I was almost raped by someone I knew and respected.

He was a lawyer. A criminal defense lawyer, and one of the best. I admired him very much, and at the age of 16, I experienced one of my first strong attractions. Certainly, my teenage hormones were raging, but I truly had no concept of the real danger women and girls face. I had no framework or foundation to understand the type of violence that happens to us so often. Most girls at that age have no idea what kind of ugliness they might have to endure at the hands of men. So, I allowed myself to innocently express my crush by flirting and teasing. He was 40 years old, handsome, and wealthy. And he was someone I saw regularly.

One evening, he invited me to his condominium before we headed out to dinner. Thinking nothing of it, I accepted, and we headed up. The heavy summer heat of Chicago clung to my skin, so the cool blast of an air conditioner was a wave of relief the moment I stepped inside. I assumed we would only be there for a few minutes, so I lingered in front of the vent, closing my eyes and letting the cold air sting against my face. For a moment, I wasn't in that apartment at all. I was back at my grandmother's house as a child, standing in front of her air conditioning unit...

Then, without warning, he came up behind me, turned me around, and started kissing me. Though I had always imagined kissing him, it was different than what I had imagined. He smoked cigarettes, so his breath was terrible. I was disgusted, but he continued to force his mouth on mine. Just as quickly as it began, he stopped. It seemed as though he recognized himself and the actions he was taking with a 16-year-old child. Then he said, "OK, I'm sorry. Look at what you do to me. You're so beautiful." I was instantly relieved, feeling that the whole ordeal was finally over and we could leave for dinner. But as soon as I exhaled, he grabbed me again and forced me into his bedroom, pushing me onto his bed. He climbed on top of me, furiously kissing and groping the private parts of my body. He was attempting intercourse. From summers spent playing outside in Mississippi and years of nonstop tennis after school, I had developed a wiry build with noticeable muscle and strength. That was the only reason I was able to fight him off and prevent him from penetrating me.

Every time he snapped and then appeared to regain his composure, he would apologize and subsequently hold me responsible for his behavior. Blamed my beauty, my body. He did this about four or five times. Back and forth. Jekyll and Hyde. From consoling me to attacking me. Back and forth. Until finally he remembered that we needed to leave. So he offered a shower. With him. And I did because it was the only way to get out of there.

I know now that it was an attempted rape. At the time, I did not realize that what had happened was a crime, whether or not he had completed the act. I also did not understand that I was a victim of trauma, that I should have sought professional help, or that I was a survivor of anything. So I stayed silent and carried on as if nothing had happened.

When I was 21, I saw him walking in downtown Chicago. You can always feel the changing seasons there. Spring rushes in on a warm, steady breeze, making walking downtown exhilarating. Each corner releases its own distinct scent. Lake water, popcorn, hot dogs, liquor, perfume, even grit. The years between 16 and 21 had carried enormous change, bringing new knowledge, experiences, and a clearer understanding of the world. By then, I could finally recognize that he had attempted to rape me and grasp what that truly meant. The air had felt light and full of possibility before I saw him. When we locked eyes, the season changed.

With my newfound understanding, I approached him differently. He suggested we step into a restaurant; I agreed, and we were seated at an outside table. I ordered a Coke; he ordered coffee. I believe he expected we'd have a pleasant conversation. He may have even believed that he still had a chance to persuade me to engage in sex. As hard as it might be to believe, he seemed to think that was appropriate. But I did not tarry long on small talk. I looked at him directly and stated, "You almost raped me." Then I added, "I was a virgin. And if I wasn't a strong kid, that would have been my first experience. You were wrong for that."

Although it was a significant moment for me, he did not seem very phased. He apologized, but not in an "I almost raped you" way. It resembled an apology you might receive for potentially embarrassing someone or failing to show up for a dinner date. I do not know if my words really affected him. But, you certainly could not tell by the way he conducted himself toward me for the next 30 years. For me, that chance meeting and the opportunity to finally tell him the truth felt like a weight had been lifted. I had kept this matter to myself, similar to how one might hide an ugly sore. So for me, the moment served its purpose. A small piece of my mind could rest.

The event happened the summer before my senior year of high school. As you can imagine, I had no time to waste on sadness, victimhood, or the usual teenage angst. Instead, I focused on making my senior year amazing, and to this day I can still say that my Hyde Park Career Academy Class of 1988 experience owes me nothing. As valedictorian, I had a charmed transition into college. Mr. Bray, my high school guidance counselor, was incredibly supportive and understood that no matter what school I chose, I would need money. He would come get me *out of class* to apply for scholarships, have me sit down to write essays, and manage my submissions so I could secure as much funding as possible.

Mr. Bray was a Black man, and I was fortunate to have him guiding me from one stage of my education to the next. I applied to four schools, including Harvard, and when the acceptance letter arrived, I was both amazed and thrilled. Few students I knew even considered the Ivy League, but I did. The reason was simple: If I was going to create change and embark on a journey that would matter to Black people, I needed a strong foundation, one that would open doors, attract attention, and stand as an unassailable qualification. I had to aim higher, take bigger steps, and go after opportunities my peers might never consider. I had to accomplish more than what my parents and family before me had achieved. I applied because I believed I was good enough. Plus, why wouldn't they take me? I was an anomaly, as I would be many more times in my career.

I applied for countless scholarships from businesses, churches, sororities, and government programs willing to support students like me. They came in chunks of $500, $1,000, $2,000, and together it all added up. My mother did not have money to fund my college education. That is a common reality in so many Black homes. In this country, it is almost impossible for a single parent with more than one child on a middle-class or lower middle-class income to save or accumulate enough for college tuition. So, while we always had everything we needed and much of what we wanted, as a family, we simply could not amass the money required for four years at an Ivy League institution. That meant I needed Harvard to give me a lot of money. I needed to take out significant loans. And I needed money from any source available, which

23

meant applying for as many scholarships as I could. Almost every time I applied or competed, I was awarded funding. Between those scholarships, the money Harvard granted me directly, and student loans, I was able to attend.

Harvard is a need-based, blind application school. This means money or ability to pay is not one of the factors required for entry. And, if you are accepted, they assist you with finances. Harvard provided me with a significant portion of its overall tuition each year in the form of grants. That is huge. And it is huge for all Black people and people who are not rich. That generosity let me go to school, which I couldn't have done without it.

Things are different now. Students today are expected to come up with big money to attend college. And long gone are the days of Pell Grants, Stafford Loans, and those student-friendly products that made the American dream a possible reality for so many. Now, getting a basic college education means either having massive amounts of cash or taking out commercial loans with high interest and co-signers often required. It is now as if one is taking out a loan for something purely personal, like a boat or house or car. National policies should encourage young scholars to continue their education and contribute meaningfully to society, but instead, they face an uphill battle with towering student loans and a life of debt. Shouldn't we do everything we can to ensure that everyone gets a higher education?

I vividly remember filling out the financial aid form for Harvard. When I got to the section that asked about parental contribution toward tuition, I ran from my bedroom to the living room to talk to my mother. I asked her how much her parental contribution was for my studies at Harvard. We had never had any such conversation before. I thought she would say a number, an amount of money, for me to fill in on this application. But my mother said that she didn't have any money and that she could not contribute to my college education. She simply didn't have it. She told me to put "0" in the section of the form that asked for parental contribution.

I was floored. It was completely surprising to me that my mother did not have any savings earmarked for my college education. Not because we talked about it or that I was told so. But because I never knew we were poor. In fact, it wasn't until that very moment that I realized we were *poor*. If someone had asked me before then, I probably would have said that we belonged to the upper middle class or something similar. I knew we were not rich, but I didn't know we were *poor*. It seriously never occurred to me that I would have to go to school on my own steam. And, with that blast of cold water, I completed the application, entering zero as the amount of parental contribution.

I view it as a tribute to my mother that I did not know we were poor. I visited my family in Mississippi and St. Louis at least twice a year. We went to the movies, concerts, amusement parks and had a little spending money. I got an allowance each week. We received Christmas and birthday presents, celebrated various holidays, and enjoyed all the things that children in America typically do. I did not know we were part of the underclass. We didn't carry ourselves that way, and my mother did not treat us like we had nothing.

Looking back, I can see how every part of my childhood—from the red dirt roads and cotton fields of Mississippi to the cramped apartment on the South Side of Chicago—shaped me. It gave me the hunger to push forward, the courage to walk into rooms I had never imagined for myself, and the determination to make my journey matter.

Chapter Four
Belonging, and the Voice It Gave Me

I might have been the poorest person in my Harvard class, but my first night was magical. I was assigned to Gray's Hall, one of the several freshman dormitories in Harvard Yard. It sits at the long end of the Yard, parallel to Massachusetts Avenue. The Yard itself is one of the most well-known freshman yards in the country. Every day, hundreds of people walk into Harvard Yard just to feel the gravitas of the place.

But, anyway, back to my first night at Harvard. As I lay in my room in Grays Hall, I looked out the window at the freshman week activities that continued late into the night, including talks, information sessions, and tours. As the evening progressed, a very special program occurred. It was called Take Back the Night. I had never heard of this concept, nor had I truly thought about rape on college campuses. This particular night, female students at Harvard marched in a kind of vigil. Each one of them had a candle in her hands as two or three students spoke about awareness and the prevalence of sexual assaults on college campuses. They talked of women standing together and supporting each other. And they talked about ways that the administration could protect female students. It was the first time I truly understood the idea of women needing protection in this world—protection from men—and the first time I saw women come together to demand that protection for one another. Witnessing that solidarity was powerful. Until then, I had carried my experiences alone, but in that moment I realized the power of collective strength. It was a turning point in how I thought about women, justice, and myself. And I loved it. It was as if Harvard's wisdom, history, and tradition could seep into you like osmosis. It was a hallowed setting, and knowing that so many brilliant minds had come before you felt empowering.

During my first week at Harvard, I was introduced to the Kuumba Singers, Harvard's oldest Black student organization and a renowned choir dedicated to celebrating Black creativity and culture. For me, they became a major source of respite, love, and protection in this new Ivy League world. It is impossible to overstate the influence this organization had on my mental and emotional health. If you have not experienced the Kuumba Singers for yourself, stop reading this book for a moment and reserve a seat at their next concert. No, I mean it. Right now.

I joined the moment I had a chance, and Kuumba instantly felt like home. The three women who became my roommates and lifelong best friends were also Kuumbabes, as we call ourselves. Every person who sang in Kuumba is dear to me. The experience was like no other. We performed three on-campus concerts each year and toured the United States by bus, singing at events and churches across the country. On one such tour, we had the honor of performing at the famous Abyssinian Baptist Church in Harlem, New York. Kuumba was where I found the acceptance that had eluded me in the "real" church, and it became the centerpiece of my Harvard experience. It was my church—the place where I felt grounded, safe, and lifted all at once. Not a church in the traditional sense, but it fulfilled that role in my life.

The brick-and-mortar churches I attended growing up were varied but never steady, and none of them ever felt like home. It was not because my mother failed to instill Christianity. She took me to church services, Bible study, and age-appropriate lessons on God and Jesus. We went to a large, progressive church under the leadership of Dr.

Johnnie Coleman, a famous female pastor on the South Side of Chicago. We also attended the Presbyterian Church by the Lake, just a block from our apartment and another from Rainbow Beach on Lake Michigan. In Mississippi, we worshiped at Antioch Baptist Church, where my family members both led the church and sat in the pews; two uncles and a great uncle pastored there across three decades, and both of my grandparents are buried in its cemetery. I had religion, but not in a fanatical or overbearing way. I knew God, and that foundation has always been important in my life. Still, in none of those churches did I ever feel truly at home.

I never officially became a member of any church, and I have not been baptized. The older I got, the more I felt like an outsider in those spaces. As a young adult, I came out as gay, which seemed to be wholly inconsistent with church and church life. Was I wrong for being gay? Was the church wrong for denouncing same-sex relationships? How can someone be both a Christian and gay? Is God judging me by who I love? Am I actually a Christian? These are the questions that I have been trying to find answers to and reconcile with my life for the last three decades. As a result, actual church membership became increasingly unlikely.

My studies of Afro-Atlantic religions contributed to my distance from the Christian church as an institution. I learned about Afro-Atlantic religions from J. Lorand Matory at Harvard as an undergraduate. I took two of his courses in the Anthropology department, even though I was a government major. One of my roommates was an anthropology major and persuaded me to take my first course with Professor Matory. This was one of the best decisions I made while at Harvard. Professor Matory is one of the most brilliant teachers I have had at any level of education. He made the study of these religions real, tangible, magical, exciting. Santeria, Vodun, Condomble, and, to some extent, Black Christianity are all syncretic religions that spawned from the African slave trade. In countries like Puerto Rico, Haiti, Cuba, and Brazil, slaves were forced to convert to Catholicism. However, in each of these locations, enslaved people found ways to secretly maintain and hold onto some of their traditional Yoruba and other African spiritual practices. The secret traditional worship combined with Catholicism created new religions altogether. Many of the Catholic saints are equated with African deities. These religions, especially Vodun ("Voodoo"), are often misunderstood by mainstream adherents. The truth is, our culture has a rich and full history that requires the study of several disciplines to understand.

After these courses with Professor Matory, I felt like Christianity was not my only option. I was convinced that I would travel to Brazil, New Orleans, and Cuba. And that I would be overtaken by one or the other deity and convert to an entirely new, African-based religion. In my mind, that seemed right. Professor Matory taught me that gay and lesbian practitioners are not shunned and are often leaders in these lesser-known religions. But that transformation has yet to occur.

I also took two other courses on religion at Harvard. One was called The Bible, and one was called Jesus. The Bible course focused on the theory that there were four different authors of the Bible. We discussed the writings at length, along with their four different styles, tones, biases, and meanings. To this day, I have not been able to have a meaningful conversation with a religious scholar about this theory. The course on Jesus centered around the many characters of Jesus. We learned of his persona as a son, a healer, a friend to the downtrodden, a leader, a politician, a caregiver, and a truth teller. The class really expanded on my limited knowledge of Jesus from sermons and Bible study. But my basic questions about Christianity were still unanswered.

And, of course, the actual church is where I experienced the most blatant and hurtful homophobia. The last time I attended church in Mississippi was in the mid-to-late 2000s, when I went to Wednesday evening Bible study. It was my family's newly built church, less than a year old, and it was my first time stepping inside. Before the service began, the pastor and my mom gave me a tour of the building. I was excited to see what my family had accomplished. Most of the congregation were Frisons who had made real sacrifices to pay for the church to be built. These were poor people, most of them working in factories or other hourly, physically demanding jobs. The building itself was an impressive, spacious sanctuary with beautiful office spaces, a modern kitchen, and plenty of room for fellowship. I was genuinely proud. When it was time for Bible study to begin, I proudly sat in the first row between my mother and my Aunt Mary.

No sooner had we sat down, the pastor started right in. First thing out his mouth was a question: had we seen that "sissy" Anderson Cooper talking 'bout something or other? I tuned out the rest. Was the pastor really saying this from the pulpit? Was I really being humiliated in church by my own uncle? It felt surreal. At that moment, I was reduced to a freak of nature. I would have gotten up and walked out if I hadn't been sitting between my mother and my Aunt Mary. So I sat through it, tuning out the ridicule, while the pastor went on to advise this all-Black congregation in the poorest state in the nation not to vote for President Obama because he had changed his position on "Don't Ask Don't Tell."

After the "Bible Study," I sat quietly fuming and humiliated on the ride home. The next day, my aunt called and invited me and my mom to lunch at a restaurant in town. When we sat down to eat, my aunt looked at me and grabbed my hand. She apologized for the pastor's (her brother's) remarks. My mother joined her in that apology.

While at Harvard, I served as president of the Kuumba Singers, wrote an article for the Harvard Crimson defending Leonard Jeffries's right to speak, was active in the Black Students Association, and became something of an activist. I found my voice. I discovered that I was persuasive and skilled at arguing a position, and I wanted to put that ability to use for those whose voices were suppressed in this country. Law school became my goal. In June 1992, on a sweltering day in Cambridge, my roommates and I graduated together, and I set off for Washington, D.C. The heat there was even more intense, but it felt good, as if the city were preparing me for the greater challenges and responsibilities that awaited me at Georgetown Law.

I arrived on 1L orientation day without ever having set foot on the Georgetown campus or in Washington, D.C. After orientation, I searched the newspaper ads for an apartment and found one at 16th and New Hampshire Street in Northwest, just behind Malcolm X Park. Washington, D.C. quickly became another city I loved, with its history, energy, and sense of purpose that seemed to match my own.

At Georgetown in 1993, there were only two Marines on campus, and one of them slipped Judge Advocate program recruitment flyers into our student mailboxes. The Judge Advocate Division is the legal branch of the Marine Corps, where attorneys serve as officers who advise commanders, prosecute and defend cases, and interpret military law. That single piece of paper sparked a curiosity that quickly grew into determination. The more I learned about the Marine Corps, the more I wanted to serve. During my second year, I was selected to attend Officer Candidate School in Quantico, and I have been a Marine ever since. Becoming a Marine remains my greatest achievement and most significant transformation. It is almost like being a vampire; once it happens, there is no return.

Alongside this new path, I worked my way through law school, spending summers split between legal work and teaching tennis to adults and children. After my third year, I worked at the Quincy District Court in Massachusetts while studying for the bar examination. In addition to those commitments, I ran Georgetown Outreach, a community service umbrella that connected students and volunteers with major service providers in Washington, D.C., including food kitchens, homeless shelters, women's shelters, and substance abuse facilities.

One of the few summer jobs I genuinely enjoyed was teaching tennis. Before law school, I had taught children, teens, and adults in Chicago for several summers, but in 1993, I started working as a children's tennis instructor at Sportsmen's Tennis Club in Boston. Sportsmen's, founded in 1961, is one of the first Black-owned tennis clubs in the United States and an important part of the city's sports history. Located in Boston's renowned Emerald Necklace, it is an 1,100-acre chain of parks and waterways designed by Frederick Law Olmsted. The club hosted a summer camp created specifically to serve inner-city youth.

In the summer of 1995, after teaching children's tennis at Sportsmen's, I joined them in a game of kickball on one of the open fields. The grounds were lovely, but the grass was full of small divots that made running risky. I didn't realize how dangerous it was until I was sprinting across it. At 24, I felt fearless and unbreakable. I started the game with my class, and soon after, my foot landed in one of those divots. I rolled my ankle, and as I went down I finally understood why they call it "rolling your ankle." The bone on the outside of my ankle actually touched the ground. I went home thinking it was just a sprain and that a little TLC would fix it. I took ibuprofen, elevated it, and iced it. After a couple of days, I could limp on it. Eventually, I was able to walk, but it never felt quite right. I did not go to the doctor. That was me at 24—invincible, or maybe just reckless.

A few weeks later, I visited my family in Mississippi. My family is extremely fun-loving, so this particular weekend, we went go-kart riding. It was a good time. But as I walked from the parking lot to the track, I stepped on a rock and rolled my ankle again. The intense pain told me that something was really wrong, so I finally went to the doctor and learned that I had torn a ligament. I was concerned that the injury would limit my running, speed, agility, etc. Fortunately, it only took several weeks of physical therapy to rehabilitate it before going onto active duty.

I also learned that as torn ligaments heal, they form scar tissue that can disrupt nearby nerves and their connection to the brain. When I stepped on that rock, my brain and ankle didn't communicate properly, and I landed badly. That breakdown is called impaired proprioception, the body's reduced ability to sense position and movement, which is essential for balance and coordination. When I was younger, I heard "old folks" say an ankle, knee, or shoulder that had once been injured would ache when rain was coming. Just a dull soreness that never lets you forget. That scar tissue stays with you for life.

The same is true for other kinds of wounds. The lingering pain of a physical assault. The emotional hurt of being ridiculed by my only uncle, a pastor, because I am part of the LGBTQ community. Some injuries are more visible than others, but they all leave their mark. We learn to live with them. They are the reminders.

It brings to mind that song, "Good Morning, Heartache," by the inimitable Billie Holiday.

US Marine Corps & The Law
Scars of Duty

Me, Active Duty USMC, 1996

Solo Practice, Frison Law Firm, P.C., 2024

Chapter Five
The Birds and the Bees

During my school-age years from 1970 to 1980, I was a tomboy who only played "boy" games and never understood the purpose of wearing a dress. But I "went with" at least two notable boys from school. From 1980 to 1990, I was basically a little cross-dresser, constantly imitating my idol, Michael Jackson, in hairstyle, clothing, and dance. But I still had boys on the brain. From 1990 to 1996, I dated men and married one in 1995 after graduating from law school. The marriage was very short-lived, separating before our second anniversary.

That summer, I had no time to waste on sadness, just as I had pushed myself to move forward after the assault that occurred before my senior year of high school. Compartmentalizing pain had become second nature, and once again, I buried myself in preparation—this time for the bar exam. During the summer of 1995, I studied relentlessly for the Massachusetts Bar Exam, and while sitting for that test, I couldn't help but contemplate what it meant to be there as a Black woman, given the history of the bar itself. Massachusetts established the first written exam, but exclusion has long defined access to the profession nationwide. For years, states offered "diploma privilege" only to men graduating from white schools or limited applicants to oral exams that could be easily manipulated. The American Bar Association (ABA), too, was once an all-white club. In 1912, when it accidentally admitted three Black lawyers, it quickly revoked their memberships. In 1925, Texas passed a law restricting law school admission to white students only, and it took a U.S. Supreme Court case, *Sweatt v. Painter*, to force the University of Texas to admit Heman Marion Sweatt. As late as 1938, the University of Missouri Law School was still justifying the exclusion of Black applicants on the grounds that admitting a "Negro" violated the state's constitution and public policy.

Knowing this history makes passing the bar more than just a personal achievement; it feels like part of a larger fight. Every time I learn how systematically the law was used to shut us out, I become even more determined to excel and prove by living example that the myth of Black underachievement is just that—a myth.

The following summer marked another turning point in my life. I was officially divorced and newly single, and everything around me seemed to shift—but this time, at my direction and with my full acceptance. Summers have always felt transformational to me. Maybe it's the heat, maybe it's the freedom, but that year carried the weight of something cinematic, like The Summer of '42. (If you don't know that movie, you may be too young to be reading this book.) It's a story about new love and the ache that comes with it, and in many ways, that was where I found myself.

I was back home in Chicago and wanted one last hurrah before starting the next chapter. At 26, newly divorced and preparing to head onto active duty with the Marine Corps that September, I intended to make the most of that summer. Chicago summers are hot—so hot that even the lake breeze can't cool you. On the South Side, you'd see glistening little Black bodies spilling out of the water at Rainbow Beach, my old stomping grounds. But that summer I was living in Hyde Park with my college roommate, Paitra, who was working on her PhD at the University of Chicago. I spent my days working remotely for Attorney Robert Willis, researching and writing, and my nights soaking in the city before my next chapter began.

One sizzling summer day, I was wandering through a street fair in Hyde Park when a woman struck up a casual conversation with me. At first I didn't think much of it. I was dressed in my usual gear: jeans, t-shirt, baseball cap, and backpack. Looking back, I probably came off a little studdish since androgyny had always been my style. As the conversation continued, I realized she was flirting with me. Before long, she asked me out.

Caught off guard, I laughed and said, "I think you've got the wrong impression." It was my polite way of letting her know she was barking up the wrong tree because I was not gay. Or at least, I did not think so. But something about her confidence, her smile, and the way she carried herself stayed with me. I found myself curious, even intrigued. That moment of hesitation made me wonder about feelings I had never fully explored.

"But was I?" would later become a running joke between us. Because it was with her, a Black Panamanian woman, that I first truly understood my love for women. We went on to share nearly seven years together.

Looking back, she wasn't even the first woman I had been attracted to. I remember having a crush on my ex-husband's cousin—while we were married. Probably not the best situation. At the time, though, I didn't recognize it as a crush. I thought it was simply an intense admiration.

By the end of the summer, there was no mistaking it: it was more than an intense admiration. I was dating a woman. And every single day that summer, I was surrounded by women. A whole new world of love and community opened up to me. We worked during the day and spent our nights partying downtown and on Chicago's North Side. All women, all the time, and I loved it. Some days I would catch my reflection in the mirror and ask, 'Who are you?' I didn't always have an answer, but I accepted who I was becoming. That summer heat returned, and with it came the feeling that love was in the air along Lake Michigan.

Chapter Six
The Big Suck

That unbothered bliss did not last the whole year. In the winter of 1996 through 1997, I began my service in the United States Marine Corps at The Basic School (TBS), better known as "The Big Suck" or "Time Between Sundays." These were just a couple of the colorful names for what was, in truth, a relentless and exhausting stretch of instruction. It was a grueling six-month program where every new officer, fresh from commissioning at Officer Candidate School, was trained in leadership, weapons, and combat tactics.

A friend's class had been the last all-male TBS company. By the time I arrived, women were fully integrated, and the ones in my class were hardcore Devil Dogs, the nickname dating back to World War I for Marines who excelled in every aspect of training.

Although I believed I was tough before joining the Marine Corps, I quickly realized that I was slower and weaker than many of my fellow trainees. I had to push myself harder, elevate my performance, and compete on a completely different level if I wanted to keep up.

It reminded me of my first days at Harvard. I had arrived on campus as the high school valedictorian only to discover that nearly everyone else had been valedictorian as well. I considered myself a badass in both settings, but at The Basic School, I found myself surrounded by nothing but badasses. Simply put, TBS was more challenging than Harvard. There was an enormous amount of training and testing packed into a very short period of time. The training included infantry tactics, weapons, leadership, good old physical training (PT), and additional punishing regimens that tested even the strongest among us—mentally and physically.

For me, the academics came more naturally. It was all new, but I was able to access and retain the information with ease. I could deliver a "shit hot" five-paragraph order, the structured operations order used in the Marine Corps to communicate mission, execution, administration, logistics, and command signals. But the physical demands of the place pushed me to my absolute limits.

One particular course, the Endurance ("E") Course, was especially brutal. A Marine named Flynn, who would soon become one of my best friends in life, was the reason I finished it. I could never say enough about him. He was literally the reason I made it through The Basic School.

At the start of the course, Flynn asked me what I wanted as my Military Occupational Specialty (MOS). I told him that I was a lawyer and wanted to serve as a judge advocate in the 4402 position. Flynn was a graduate of the United States Naval Academy. At the time, I did not fully understand what that meant, but later learned it meant that he was already in top physical condition and deeply familiar with the Marine Corps' protocols, customs, and practices long before arriving at TBS with me.

Flynn actually seemed impressed that I had attended law school, passed the Massachusetts bar exam, and was present with him as we went through the second part of what felt like Marine Corps harassment training for officers. But I was the one who was impressed. And at that time, I didn't realize just how much I should look up to this Marine.

The Endurance Course was an 8-mile run in boots, utilities, a helmet, and a weapon that we were required to finish within 80 minutes to pass. The course wound through the woods of Quantico, Virginia, and included walls, ropes, cargo nets, and other obstacles to add to the lovely trail run. It was the longest distance I had ever run and the furthest I had ever even wanted to run. Each attempt wore me out. I started running it on weekends in preparation for the eventual test because during every attempt, I failed to finish within the allotted time. Eventually, Flynn joined me on Saturdays to run it with me.

Saturdays at TBS were your own, a time for a young officer to be unobserved briefly, to do some shopping, soaking, recuperating, socializing, studying, and preparing for the next week. To give up time and energy to help another Marine get it the fuck together was huge. He pushed me, but with compassion, which is not an easy combination to master. And that was just one event that Flynn got me through.

In the field, Flynn was an ally at all times. We were assigned to Fox Company at TBS, one of several training companies named using the phonetic alphabet. Fox Company is notorious for its winter weather training. Virginia is south, but not far enough to escape the cold. Winter reigned supreme there. We spent days and weeks in the field practicing offense, defense, and tactics. The days were grueling in the freezing conditions, with nothing but foxholes to sleep in and no fires allowed for tactical purposes.

Of all the challenges I faced in the Marine Corps, the most difficult for me was swim qualification. Since I wasn't going into infantry or aviation, I only needed to pass the basic level: treading water, swimming a short distance, dragging another Marine across the pool, and jumping from a 15-foot platform. I had taught myself to swim at the YMCA before training, and I could manage all the requirements except for the jump itself. I did it once while practicing but could never bring myself to do it again. To this day, I still do not know why.

I spent hours and hours and hours in the pool at TBS. Remedial swim every weekend. Humiliated. Anxious. Depressed. And what worsened it was the creeping thought that I was becoming a statistic—because Black folks can't swim, right? All because I couldn't jump off that damn platform.

I had passed every other requirement for graduation and was ready to move on to Naval Justice School and finally join the Fleet Marine Corps, i.e. active duty. But I could not do so without passing the swim qualification. I tried everything, and my friends tried everything they could to help me. Alcohol, Valium, even attempts to push me off the platform. Nothing worked. As a result, I did not graduate with my class. Instead, I was placed in a remedial company for "broken" officers and remained there for a few months.

Yes, we called the Marines in that company broken. Most of them had shin splints, a broken leg, a stress fracture, or some other injury that kept them from graduating with their class. They stayed behind to heal, to recover, to push through whatever was holding them back.

I was devastated to be among them. My body wasn't broken. Nothing was physically wrong with me. My struggle was in my mind, and that made it even harder to explain, even harder to accept. I kept thinking, "I am a Marine. Marines don't fail. Marines don't break." But there I was, labeled as broken. Stuck. Watching everyone else move forward while I stayed behind. I seriously considered giving up and leaving active duty. I felt like I had failed before I had even really begun. I had failed to be what I believed a real Marine was supposed to be.

Finally, Marine Captain Sweitzer offered to help me. I hadn't known him before this, but he was an instructor for Mike Company, working to prepare officers to move on to the Fleet Marine Corps. Despite not knowing me well, he became determined to get me through TBS. I listened and followed his lead as he gathered crates and guided me, step by step, to the pool diving board until I reached the required height of 15 feet. It was incredible, and I could not thank him enough. From the beginning, he seemed confident that it would work, and he carried it out with graciousness and professionalism. That is how Marines are. As small as the Corps is, some Marines are with you only for a season. We did not become friends. He was an infantry officer, a grunt, and I never saw him again.

Passing the swim test and graduating TBS allowed me to join the Fleet, as we used to say, officially beginning my active duty from 1997 to 2000. I had requested California, Hawaii, and overseas billets, but I was instead assigned to Marine Corps Air Station New River in Jacksonville, North Carolina. I lived at Topsail Beach and ran the air station's prosecutorial office, serving as trial counsel—the Marine Corps term for prosecutor. At this location, there was only one prosecutor, one defense counsel, and one legal assistance officer at any given time. That meant I was responsible for handling the prosecutions of all 15 helicopter squadrons on base. Military prosecutions differ from civilian ones: the unit commander, known as the convening authority, decides whether to prosecute and can impose lesser punishments. Only after that decision does the case move to trial counsel. And that was my job.

So what happens when I, the prosecuting lawyer, and the commanding officer, convening authority, disagree as to whether someone should be prosecuted or how they are prosecuted? Well, I found out firsthand what happened.

Chapter Seven

The Powers That Be

In 1999, I received a legal services package request from one of the squadrons at Marine Corps Air Station, New River. A request like this was routine and the standard way for a squadron to ask the trial counsel to draft charges against a Marine. Unlike civilian courts, the Marine Corps does not use a cookie-cutter indictment where you simply insert a name into boilerplate language. Instead, a trial counsel must write the charges and draft a paragraph that describes the alleged illegal conduct. There is some template language, but I was responsible for crafting language that accurately captured the alleged and provable conduct found in the package.

One request for legal services required me to conduct an Article 32 hearing on allegations of attempted rape and assault and battery by a Marine gunnery sergeant. He worked in what we called a short MOS, meaning few Marines in the Corps held his specialty. Because of that, Marines in short MOS fields were often given a little more protection. The Corps also sent these Marines on 'floats,' deployments lasting six or seven months at sea. During a float, Marines might travel through the Mediterranean or other regions where the Corps regularly patrols. The accused Marine had been on such a float.

When ships dock at foreign ports, it gives Marines a chance to have dinner, sightsee, and socialize. According to the report, this ship docked in Spain, where all Marines were required to follow the buddy system: they could not leave the ship or walk alone but had to remain with at least one other Marine at all times. I have never been to Spain, but I was told that dinner is typically served much later there than in the United States. So it was not surprising that the events in question took place late at night, while the streets of Palma de Mallorca were still full of people.

A gunnery sergeant broke the buddy system rule and left the ship alone. At approximately 3:00 a.m., several people on the roof deck of an apartment building saw a man dragging a woman into a vacant lot by her hair. They described him attempting to pull her clothing off. The witnesses shouted down for him to stop, and as soon as the man realized he had been seen, he ran away. The good Samaritans helped the woman call the police.

When the police arrived, the woman explained that she had been walking home after having dinner with friends. She noticed a man following her and tried to walk faster, but he sped up as well. Finally, he ran up behind her, grabbed her, and began dragging her toward the vacant lot. Based on her account, the police immediately began searching the area for the attacker. They found him only a few blocks away, shirtless and running through the streets of Palma. It was the gunnery sergeant. The woman identified him on the spot, telling police that she would never forget his large, prominent eyes. The gunny was held by Spanish police but later released to the custody of the Marine Corps for prosecution.

An Article 32 hearing is comparable to a grand jury investigation. It determines whether there is enough evidence for a service member to be tried at a general court-martial, the most serious level of military trial. It functions like a preview of the trial, with witnesses and evidence presented to an investigating officer. The investigating officer must be independent: not involved in the case, not one of the base's assigned lawyers, and not under the authority of the commander who ordered the hearing.

When I received the request for legal services, I got right to work. One major challenge in this prosecution was the location of the event and witnesses. I was in Jacksonville, North Carolina, and everyone I needed to talk to was in Spain or elsewhere. My first task was to speak to the victim who was from Palma. The police report I received was relatively detailed, and I was able to reach her over the phone. I could tell she was still shaken and disturbed by the attack, but she never wavered in her commitment to seeing it through and doing her part to make sure that this Marine was prosecuted for what he did.

The convening authority in this case was a lieutenant colonel, the commander of a helicopter squadron that flew CH-46s. There were 15 different types of squadrons on the air station, which meant 15 commanding officers serving as convening authorities. Each had their own leadership style and philosophy about discipline, and I dealt with them weekly to prosecute cases. Sometimes the relationships were good, and sometimes they were not.

In my newly acquired attempted rape case, I wasted no time preparing the Article 32. Everything proceeded as planned until the day of the hearing, when I had to transport the victim from Spain to North Carolina for her testimony. It was rare to bring an overseas witness for an attempted rape case. And as a relatively new lawyer, it felt significant. The opposing counsel was the only defense attorney on the air station, a Marine officer from the Joint Law Center where I also worked. We regularly faced off against each other.

At the Article 32 hearing, the victim was clearly traumatized but firmly identified the gunny as her attacker. Her testimony, supported by eyewitness accounts and the quick arrest by Palma police, made the case strong. The investigating officer agreed, finding the testimony credible and recommending that the matter be sent to a general court-martial. I was in full agreement with that opinion.

So off I went to speak to the commanding officer of the unit. I was a captain, and he was a lieutenant colonel. Not only did he outrank me, but he was a whole different breed of officer. Nevertheless, even at my relatively young age, I considered myself an expert in criminal law, and I did not take kindly to anyone pulling rank on me when it came to my area of expertise.

In his office, the lieutenant colonel sat composed, his white and khaki uniform crisp and neatly pressed. From the start of our meeting to the end, he tried to convince me that this case should not go to a general court-martial and should not be prosecuted as an attempted sexual assault. We spent the better part of two hours discussing the case. I put forward all of my arguments based upon my knowledge of criminal law and my assessment of the strength of the case. I explained how credible the victim was. I explained that we had a strong case because the gunny was caught quickly and there were several witnesses. I tried my best to convince the lieutenant colonel to sign off on the order authorizing a court-martial against the gunny for the offenses I had drafted. He flat out refused. Not only did he pull rank, but he also took the matter totally out of my hands.

The evidence supported charges of attempted rape, indecent assault, and assault and battery. But the commanding officer only wanted to charge the gunny with violation of the buddy system order. In fact, he did not really want a prosecution at all. The lieutenant colonel told me that he was going to handle the Marine using nonjudicial punishment, also known as NJP.

Nonjudicial punishment is a proceeding available to a commanding officer whose Marine has committed an offense for which the commander does not want him to go to trial. It is reserved for lower-level offenses. The commanding officer can hear the matter, decide guilt or innocence, and impose a limited set of punishments. A commanding officer cannot send someone to jail but can restrict their movement, take money from their paycheck, or reduce their rank. NJP was a serious slap on the wrist. Certainly not the punishment expected for an allegation of this nature. To say that

I was mad, to say that I was livid, would be a gross understatement.

As a woman, it was clear to me that the commander was not taking this incident seriously. The Palma police and the Spanish government had trusted us to prosecute the Marine. He could easily have been prosecuted in Spain. As a lawyer, I was furious that a non-lawyer was able to make this decision despite my sound counsel. If I was not going to tell him how to fly his helicopters, he had no business telling me which cases to try, which charges to draft, or how to prosecute crimes. And as a captain of Marines, I was angry that he was pulling rank.

I gave him the appropriate courtesies and left his office and squadron. I went straight to my superior and told him exactly what happened and added that I was not going to stand for it. It was not fair to the victim, and it just was not right. As a Marine, I was offended at the injustice. My boss agreed with me, but his hands were tied by the commander's decision. He invited me to go over the commander's head and request that the wing commander take over the case.

In the Marine Corps, a higher commander can take a case from a lower commander and handle it himself with his own convening power. That happens in rare cases, usually when there is a serious disagreement between a wing commander and a squadron commander. It was a bold move on my part, and not one I would recommend for those seeking upward mobility in the Marine Corps, but I did not care. My integrity and my duties as a prosecutor outweighed my personal ambition for promotion. I was determined to do what I believed was right.

I drafted a letter and included a package of information about the case, which I sent to the Wing Commander at Marine Corps Air Station in Cherry Point, North Carolina. The Wing Commander invited me to meet with him and discuss the matter. During our meeting, I gave him my impressions of the case and my advice as to how it should be prosecuted, which was in line with the investigating officer's assessment and recommendation. I also detailed my discussion with the squadron commander and requested that the colonel take charge of the situation to ensure proper handling.

He did not. The colonel listened, consoled, and empathized, but he did not take the case away from the squadron or bring it to a general court-martial. I could not understand how this injustice was allowed to stand. I was floored that the powers that be did not act upon the moral obligation we had to the victim of this crime. The ordeal left me exhausted and disillusioned with military justice. I was ashamed to be a cog in the wheel that denied that woman her day in court against her attacker, and I was angry that the accused's MOS and the esteem with which he was held by the commander got in the way of a criminal prosecution.

That squadron commander reduced the case to a nonjudicial punishment for violating the buddy system. So, on record, that was all that happened: a Marine left the ship and walked alone through the beautiful streets of Palma de Mallorca on a warm night

Despite the bitterness of that assault case, my time in the Marine Corps was precious. When I left active duty in 2000, I carried both pride in my service and frustration at its failures. The lack of accountability in that case weighed heavily on me, and I could not let go of the injustice I had witnessed. I knew I had to do something about it.

In 2000, I had the opportunity to testify before the Cox Commission, a panel convened to review the Uniform Code of Military Justice (UCMJ) on its 50th anniversary. The UCMJ is the body of law that governs all military crimes, punishments, and procedures, essentially the Bible of military justice. I told the Commission the system needed to change. Even in the military setting, charging decisions should be made by a neutral prosecutor, not by commanders who were not lawyers and who had close ties to their Marines. I did not disparage commanders, because they are crucial to warfighting, but I argued that their role and the absence of legal training made for a poor mix when it came to justice.

The Commission had invited testimony from service members, lawyers, and the public. I flew from Boston to Washington, D.C., to add my voice to the many calling for change, hoping that the injustice I had witnessed would help spark reform.

I was young, a true believer in the goodness of the United States, and proud of both my service and my testimony. Most of my relationships were built on mutual admiration, many of which became lifelong friendships. One of my favorite NCOs at Marine Corps Air Station New River Joint Law Center, who had a significant impact on me, later wrote this note:

"Just want to tell you I am in awe of your lifetime accomplishments. Not surprised in the least, but just—wow. I've thought about you so much over the years, and I don't think I ever took the time to tell you what an impact you had on me as a young Marine and young man. Your emotional intelligence and awesome sense of humor shaped the way I would lead for the rest of my time in the Marines, and it kept me grounded throughout my career (and during some dark times) with the SEALs and intelligence agencies. Also, you showed up at my wedding on Long Island and wrote me the fattest check ever. I'm still so thankful for everything and proud to call you a mentor, colleague, friend, ma'am, and my favorite... Your Honor!"

Goosebumps.

Chapter Eight

Coming Up and Coming Out

So much happened in 2000, a year when many believed the turn of the century might bring the end of the world. I spent New Year's Eve in the French Quarter of New Orleans, because if Y2K was the end, I wanted to go out partying. The world kept turning, though, and thankfully a new chapter of my life was beginning.

In June, I received an honorable discharge from the United States Marine Corps, officially marking the end of my active duty. Coastal Carolina was sticky and humid, so I was happy to leave the Corps and head for the cooler climate of Boston.

I also came out to my family that year. My sister said, "Girl, please. We knew that already." My ex-husband, a Boston police officer, said he knew too. So, apparently, I had only been closeted during my time on active duty, serving under "Don't Ask, Don't Tell," one of the silliest LGBTQ policies of my lifetime. But by the time I was discharged, I was determined never to hide who I was again. The only opinions that truly mattered to me were my sister's and my mother's. My mother told me that although she did not agree because of her religious beliefs, nothing would change between us. And that was all that mattered.

That fall, I was personally hired by Tom Dwyer and the partners of the former Dwyer & Collora firm located in the prestigious Federal Reserve building at South Station in Boston. The firm was a 25-lawyer outfit with a stellar reputation for representing entities and individuals in white-collar criminal cases. The top partner and rainmaker took a chance by hiring me, the first Black lawyer to work at the firm, who is also a gay Marine from Chicago. This would also be a life-changing experience.

Many law firms wanted a docile, broken-in associate from another firm who would tolerate long, tedious projects and endless document reviews, satisfied with any tangential piece of a case as long as the pay was six figures. But Tom saw something different. He recognized that my skills were transferable to the civilian arena, and he understood that hiring his first Black associate would strengthen the firm in ways that went beyond casework or billable hours. That early experience reminded me that authenticity has value. The very things that made me different were not liabilities; they were strengths.

I was also the first associate to request health coverage for my same-sex partner, and the firm granted it with no pushback. That marked the beginning of my quest to be fully out. Once I left the Marine Corps, I resolved never to hide that part of myself again, and I have lived by that commitment.

As soon as I arrived at the firm, I originated a case. Meaning I was the one who brought it in. That was unusual for a junior associate, since most spend their days doing document production in windowless rooms. But again, I was not a typical junior associate. As a Marine lawyer, I was accustomed to presenting cases from beginning to end. Document review was not for me. I tried it briefly and hated it, so I set my sights on handling the kinds of cases I actually wanted to work on.

His name was Brad. He called me out of the blue one afternoon, and what he shared was almost unbelievable. He said he was on the run from the police and told me to check the newspaper for the story. The headline described a theft of weapons and a deadly shootout in Chicago's Union Station. Brad wasn't in Chicago, but his partners were, and the fallout was closing in fast. He knew it was bad. That's when he asked me to take his case.

We spoke again not long after that first call, and during our second conversation, I agreed to represent him. Once the decision was made, we arranged to meet in person. Because of his situation, Brad had no vehicle and couldn't risk public transportation. And since I didn't want him coming through security at the Federal Reserve building where I worked, we agreed to meet at Logan Airport in Boston later that afternoon.

It was the middle of winter; snow was already on the ground, and more was still falling. The weather was terrible, but I needed to get Brad to the state of Maine. I had told him to bring $20,000 with him to retain me. To my surprise, he brought it all in cash and traveler's checks. So there I was, in a snowstorm at Logan Airport, on the way to Maine with a fugitive and $20,000 in my BMW Z3—a convertible, no less. It was gritty work, but I loved it. Everything about the situation was suspect, but somehow we made it to the State Police barracks in Bangor, Maine where we met with the Assistant U.S. Attorney and the lead detective.

Brad and I went into the barracks and sat in a cold, old conference room. There, he told them quite a story. It went like this.

Brad was 24 years old, white, and from Minnesota. A black belt in taekwondo, he had been a popular instructor in his hometown of Minneapolis. He also had a passion for flying and landed his first job with a commercial airline. But the pay was low, barely in the $20,000s for new pilots. For a young man with talent, discipline, and a promising future, it was difficult to understand why he would involve himself in something that could put him on the run and possibly send him to prison. The answer, as I learned, started with a part-time job.

While pursuing his pilot's license, Brad worked part-time in a Minneapolis restaurant to make extra money. That was where he met a man named Daniel. As their friendship grew, Daniel bragged about buying rifles, motorcycles, and expensive cars. Since they were both bussing tables, Brad was curious about how Daniel was affording such things. Daniel admitted that he and some friends were pulling "missions" that brought in big money. Simply put, the group was robbing drug dealers. Brad was intrigued. He was young, restless, and frustrated with his low-paying pilot's job. Almost immediately, he wanted in.

Now there were four of them: Brad, Daniel, Christopher, and James. Daniel and Christopher were from California and planned to return there eventually. James knew the local drug trade in Maine, pointing out who to hit and estimating what they stood to gain. And then there was Brad, who had happened to run into Daniel in Minneapolis. What were the odds that these four men would meet, let alone come together for a criminal enterprise? But link up they did, over and over.

On their "rips," the group would storm the home or stash house of a known dealer. They wore bulletproof vests labeled DEA, carried night vision goggles and two-way radios, and came armed with a stockpile of weapons. To their victims, it looked like a real DEA raid. And because the targets were drug dealers, they never reported the crimes. During some of the rips, the group would also rough up the dealer and anyone else who was present. Brad joined them on at least three missions before things got out of control.

This last rip was the reason Brad sought my counsel. They had pulled a job in Bangor, Maine, and rolled up on their target to demand money and drugs. This time, the dealer claimed to have neither. During the exchange, someone from the crew struck the dealer with a hammer. In desperation, he told them about an auction house nearby that held a cache of guns.

The group took the bait and piled into a truck Brad had rented at Logan Airport. With Brad driving, they forced the dealer to guide them to the auction house. Once there, they shoved him out of the truck and broke in. Just as promised, the place was filled with guns—handguns, shotguns, and long rifles. The men grabbed bag after bag and carried them to the truck.

While they were hauling weapons and taking trips back and forth, a Massachusetts state trooper happened to drive past on patrol. He noticed the truck and the open door of the auction house. The group saw him too. The four men scattered into the woods, each heading in a different direction. No one took the truck.

This was a disaster for Brad. Not only had he rented the truck, but he had also left his wallet and pilot's license inside. Even though the trooper didn't catch them that night, he had Brad's full identity and a trail to follow. Still, Brad ran through the woods alone, disoriented and freezing. The truth was he wasn't even dressed for the cold or for running. To make matters worse, he was unfamiliar with the area, having only visited the state a few times with the group, and there was never a plan for emergencies. Fortunately, he stumbled onto a nearby house, knocked on the door, and told the owner his car had broken down further down the road. They let him use the phone, and he called a cab. The driver picked him up, took his cash, and dropped him at the train station, where he caught an Amtrak headed to New York.

That's why I raced him to the police station in Maine. I knew my guy was dead to rights—his ID, the rental car, everything pointed straight at him. My goal was simple: be the first one of their crew to cooperate and get the best deal possible for this very young man who had taken a terribly wrong turn.

While Brad was trying to slip out of Maine, his partners were trying to get out too. Daniel and Chris decided to head for California by train. The problem was they paid for their tickets in cash, which raised red flags with transit police. The men boarded the train unaware of how suspicious they already looked. The trip had a layover in Chicago, and that is where authorities caught up with them.

Daniel was a hothead. He had bragged constantly about going out in a blaze before ever going back to jail. He was always armed and never shy about letting people know it. So instead of answering when a police officer at Union Station asked where they were headed, Daniel pulled a Glock from his waistband. Officers drew their weapons. Daniel fired first, hitting a female officer in the leg. She went down but returned fire, striking him in the chest and killing him instantly. Chris dropped his weapon, threw up his hands, and was immediately cuffed. The officer survived. And now the game was up.

The Assistant U.S. Attorney could have thrown the book at Brad, especially after learning of the shootout in Chicago. It was a nationwide case with dozens of weapons, and he had plenty of leverage. But he was fair. He agreed to work with Brad in exchange for full cooperation, helping law enforcement piece together the crew's previous crimes. Brad was taken into custody in Maine and started serving time right away.

Back then, federal sentencing guidelines were in full effect, and I had to learn them fast. They were like a puzzle, with factors that could raise or lower the numbers. Brad had some things working for him: no prior record, full cooperation, and a prosecutor willing to see that he wasn't the leader of this ragtag crew. In the end, the government reduced the charges and even lowered the number of weapons attributed to him so his sentence calculation would come down.

By the time we stood before the judge in federal court, we had a deal: seven years in a federal facility. It took negotiations, motions, and more than a few come-to-Jesus meetings. I didn't want him to go to prison, but I knew that part was inevitable. The only question was for how long.

In the days that followed, journalists pieced together their version of events. *The Boston Globe*, the largest and most influential daily newspaper in Boston, reported:

"A Sanford man involved in a December burglary at a Lebanon auction house has pleaded guilty to a number of drug-related robberies and burglaries in York County, authorities said. The crime spree culminated in a burglary at Gateway Auctions on Dec. 9 and eventually led to a deadly shootout with police in Chicago. Police believe the group took $30,000 from Gateway Auctions."

That was the public record. But Brad had already told me far more than the papers could ever print.

Interestingly, during the course of representing Brad, I learned that the rest of the crew considered themselves white supremacists. That part of the case threw me for a loop. It felt icky working on behalf of someone tied to that, and I wondered if Brad felt the same. But the better part of me reminded myself that he had chosen me, a Black woman, to represent him. I do not believe that choice had anything to do with race. I did not represent the other men, but even so, the thought lingered in the back of my mind like a prickly annoyance.

I actually talked this over with one of the partners at the firm, a criminal defense lawyer I deeply respected. I asked her what she thought about representing someone who might hold a worldview completely opposite from my own. She told me bluntly that we do not get to pick all the attributes of our clients, and that those attributes cannot always be the basis for taking or refusing a case. She said I was a criminal defense lawyer, and that meant I would represent people who were cruddy, misguided, and sometimes downright evil. I needed to have the stomach for it.

I took that advice to heart. I carried it with me into every case I handled, representing people accused of murder, rape, robbery, and everything in between. And I managed to do it with vigor and integrity, no matter what the offense. That is exactly what criminal defense lawyers are called to do. I grew up in the law surrounded by the best of them. From Chicago to Boston to the Marine Corps, I had known some of the finest attorneys to ever practice, and I wanted to be counted among them. The next criminal trial I handled at the firm was a double murder. And I was ready.

Chapter Nine

Unbroken

I left civilian life in the winter of 2003 to serve a one-year tour in support of the War on Terror. I spent six months of that tour at Camp Smith in Hawaii and lived on base at Pearl Harbor.

It was a magical place. Just being present with the USS Arizona and USS Utah memorials, ships sunk during the 1941 attack, was phenomenal and inspiring. I was in awe of the current-day ships, the submarines, the destroyers. Pearl Harbor was beautiful—palm trees, 1940s-style houses, ocean views. I felt proud to be part of the service there.

At Camp Smith, I was assigned to the G-5 War Plans Branch, working with Marine officers who liaised with partner nations in the South Pacific. I had to obtain a Top Secret clearance, and even the temporary approval took months to process. Once secured, I was given two major tasks. The first was planning the Senior Level Seminar, a biennial conference between U.S. generals and Japanese generals from the Ground Self-Defense Force. A huge, stressful job for a captain who had never planned or even attended one before. Camp Smith was top-heavy with colonels and generals. There were hardly any company-grade officers like me, and even fewer Black Marines. Still, I dug in to work.

Once in Tokyo, I worked with my Japanese counterparts, who were doing the same job for their generals. We were stressed but excited, meeting over meals, trading gifts, and building the relationships that made the event work. Generals, though, are like little presidents. They have their staff, cars, planes, bases, lawyers, and budgets. Figuring out the hierarchy was daunting, but protocol officers helped. I also had to handle the tedious jobs like herding PowerPoint slides from each officer and making sure nothing classified was included without proper clearance.

Outside of the conference, I managed the generals' daily activities, evening dinners, and their spouses' events. I got close with hotel staff to keep everything running and within budget. It was fascinating and exhausting work.

I literally knew one person on the island, but I knew her pretty well, and we had a very tight bond. We had trained together at Officer Candidate School in the same platoon, then later I hired her through the Marine for Life program, a service that placed reservist officers around the country to help Marines transition back into civilian life. She was a Black woman, and I was excited to be working with her. In Hawaii, she was already doing that work and walked me through their process. She even had an apartment off base in a beautiful neighborhood. For a while, that connection helped me feel less alone, but it wasn't enough to shield me from the isolation and bias I would face at Camp Smith.

I did not bring a car with me to Hawaii, and I was determined to have my own way to get around. So I decided to learn to ride a motorcycle. I rented one for practice, then signed up for a motorcycle course at a community college on the Windward side of the island. For a week straight, I was out in a huge parking lot with twenty others, riding little Ninja 200s, learning the rules of the road and how to handle a bike. By the end of that week, I had my M class license. A week later, I had a motorcycle.

My bike wasn't flashy. It was more like something Fonzie from *Happy Days* would ride. An older gentleman in Honolulu sold it to me. He had a few bikes and a little legal trouble, so we struck a deal: I'd give him some money and help him out pro hac vice on a minor case. It felt like a win for both of us.

At first, I loved the bike. Riding every day through Honolulu streets, past palm trees and ocean views, felt like freedom. But it didn't take long to realize he sold me a piece of junk. More than once, while I was cruising through traffic or out on the highway, the thing would suddenly lose all power. No throttle, no control—just coasting to a dead stop in the middle of busy roads. Scary doesn't even begin to cover it. I kept hauling it back to the mechanic. He tinkered, patched, jerry-rigged, but the problem never went away. Finally, he admitted what I already knew: he couldn't fix it.

I went back to the seller and asked him to take the bike back. He refused but offered me an old car instead. I didn't want that. We reached a standoff.

And then he did the unthinkable. He wrote a complaint to my command.

That's one of the worst things someone can do to you while you're serving on active duty—send a letter accusing you of violating ethics. His complaint said I had failed to follow through on his case. A handwritten note with no investigation, no context, it landed on the desk of my commanding officer, a lieutenant colonel who had never even met me.

I was summoned and ordered to stand at attention and chewed out like I was guilty. No questions were asked. Then he forwarded the note to the staff judge advocate (SJA), who called me in with his deputy. When they offered me a chair, I stayed standing. I knew what kind of meeting it was.

They lectured me about practicing law in Hawaii without a license. I explained my plan: to appear pro hac vice, with a local attorney's sponsorship, something done all the time. I was in good standing in my state. I had lawyers ready to sign. But they didn't care. They weren't interested.

They wrote up a report saying I had violated ethics rules. I wrote my response, saying bias was at play. I was a young, Black, female captain, brand new to the command, being judged on the basis of one civilian's handwritten complaint. Eventually, the SJA higher-up reviewed it and said it was just a technical violation, no further action. But the damage was done.

Camp Smith was already a challenging environment, dominated by colonels and generals who were predominantly white and male. As one of the few captains, and one of even fewer Black officers, I felt watched, judged, and excluded. My only contact with my commanding officer was that one angry meeting. My only contact with the other lawyers was through that investigation. That was it.

I had volunteered to come to Hawaii, thinking I could contribute something useful during my year away from Boston. Instead, I was isolated.

It's hard to describe the weight of it. The looks, the silence, the questions that never came with answers. The absence of invitations. The way I was made to feel unwelcome. That became the scar.

And yet, all of it was set against Oahu—the greenest, lushest, most stunning place I've ever seen. Palm trees, endless beaches, perfect weather. To this day, the island is precious to me. But the turmoil I endured at Camp Smith clouded it, and that scar has stayed with me.

Fast forward to the summer of 2004. Summer again, I know. After the lemon I bought in Honolulu, I got another motorcycle, a Kawasaki Ninja 600. When I left the island, I shipped it from Pearl Harbor to Boston. And, later that summer, promptly crashed it into a streetlight pole at the corner of Charles and Beacon Streets, just a few miles from my house in Dorchester. Another scar, another story.

Luckily, I wasn't totaled in the accident, but I was badly injured. And it was my fault. I had gone out alone to one of my favorite house music scenes. One helmet. Met a woman. And you know, bad stories often start that way. She wanted me to take her back to her school in Cambridge. It was early in the night, and I was smart enough to say no. I told her I didn't have an extra helmet and made all the reasonable arguments against the idea. A few hours and a few drinks later, I was agreeing to that ride.

I gave her my helmet—brilliant, I know—and we took off. We didn't make it more than three or four blocks before I hit a traffic light pole. The pole won. We both hit the pavement. Thank God she wasn't seriously hurt. I wasn't so lucky. I ended up with a burst bladder. Yes, it is exactly as painful as it sounds. What I didn't know until months later is that the injury is 50% fatal.

I was rushed into emergency surgery at Mass General Hospital. I had never even broken as much as a finger before, but now I was laid up with a life-threatening injury. Stellar doctors saved my life.

It took a little time to heal, to get back on my feet, to run, work, and ride again. And when I did, I bought a newer, bigger bike—a Kawasaki Z1000—as soon as I could I refused to stop riding. I refused to be broken. We are not broken. We may be battered, bruised, scarred, but never broken.

Chapter Ten

Guilty

My first murder case was a double murder. The crime took place on Castlegate Road in Boston, right in the heart of Roxbury. That neighborhood was dense, rough, and known for violence. Castlegate itself has a reputation for drugs and families who had been selling for generations. When the chance came to try the double murder, I did not hesitate.

One summer night, an uncle, his brother, and his brother's son were sitting in a car on Castlegate Road when shots rang out. The father and son died where they sat. The uncle survived, even after being hit eight times. It was a brazen, brutal attack, and my client, Renardo Williams, was charged with the crime.

Renardo knew the victims. He had grown up with the uncle, and at one point they were rivals in the drug trade. But Renardo had been locked up for years on an armed assault and had only recently returned to the neighborhood. He was living with his fiancée and their daughter, trying to build a life.

The survivor told police the shooter wore a dreadlock wig but said he still recognized him as Renardo because he had known him for years. Learning that he was accused of the crime, Renardo went on the run and headed up to the state of Maine. While there, he went back to what he knew: selling drugs. He got caught in a sting, sold to an informant, and was promptly busted with two kilos of cocaine. Maine charged him with trafficking, then turned him over to Massachusetts to face the murder charges first.

Before taking the case, I did not know anything about the Castlegate area or the family who ran it. Once I took it, I spent hours on that street, just watching. The buildings, the people, the comings and goings. Trying to pick up on anything the police had missed that could help me fight these indictments.

The survivor told the story this way: he was behind the wheel, his brother in the passenger seat, his nephew in the back. In the side mirror he saw a man walking down the middle of the street, wearing a wig. He said to himself, "Why does Renardo have on that wig?" Then shots rang out. Bullets tore through the car, hitting every passenger.

When the smoke cleared, the father and son were dead. The brother had been hit eight times but lived to testify.

Hearing it, I thought about how terrifying it must have been. My mind went back to live fire training in the Marine Corps. The sound of rounds ripping, muzzles flashing, the smell of gunpowder in the air. Except in training, I knew no bullet would hit me. Sitting trapped in a car with shots exploding all around you? That is a different kind of hell.

The trial was held on the eighth floor of Suffolk Superior Court. My first trial in Superior Court. That courthouse is old, dark, and unfriendly. The wood paneling makes the halls feel heavy. It is where many of Boston's most serious cases play out, and where too many people have been sentenced to life. I did not want Renardo to become just like the others.

I thought he was a good kid at heart. He came from struggle. In neighborhoods like that, selling drugs or running with a crew as a teenager does not automatically make you a bad person. It means you are surviving. Renardo had a fiancée, a daughter, and another baby on the way. He had gotten his CDL license and wanted to drive trucks. He wanted to provide. But now he was back in custody, staring down two counts of murder and one count of attempted murder.

The evidence against him was thin. No gun. No wig. No forensics. No other witnesses. Just one man's testimony. Today we know eyewitness testimony is some of the weakest evidence there is. But back then, it was treated like gold. And for whatever reason, the survivor was determined to say that Renardo did it. Maybe he believed it. Maybe it was revenge. Maybe it was payback from their old rivalry. Either way, I had to dismantle it.

The crime scene photos were brutal. Blood everywhere in the car. The autopsy pictures were worse. Once strong men lying cold on steel tables, looking so small. The holes in their bodies seemed almost too small to kill, but there they were. Life snatched away.

I did not believe the survivor. Renardo and I thought he had his reasons for pointing the finger, and none of them had to do with the truth. That block was tiny. Castlegate was one street long, yet it carried so much history, so much violence. To me, the whole case came down to the survivor's credibility.

Every lawyer knows that the closing argument is where you make your money in a trial. In Massachusetts, a first-degree murder conviction means life without parole. Period. The judge has no discretion. Everything was on the line, so I gave it all I had. I preached, I pleaded, I even tap danced. I called the survivor a liar to his face. He was in the front row, and when I said it, he shot me the finger and stormed out. I expected worse, but he left it at that. I kept going.

When the jury went out, I tried not to guess. You never really know. But waiting is torture. You pace, you reassure your client, you replay every detail in your head.

They were gone for two days. Then the verdict came. NOT GUILTY. My first murder case, and I had won it! I had saved my client from life in prison. I cannot describe that feeling. Happiness does not cover it. Relief, joy, gratitude, all mixed together. I gave the closing I would want someone to give for me if I were the one on trial. And I left it all on the field.

But Renardo wasn't finished with the system, and the system wasn't finished with him. Massachusetts had acquitted him, but Maine still had him on trafficking charges. It was a federal case, and they meant to make an example out of him. I packed up and headed north into a federal courtroom where the sentencing guidelines were the harshest I had ever seen. They had him cold with one kilo on him another that they found and attributed to him.

Because Renardo had been caught in a sting with two kilos of cocaine, federal court meant double digits. Mandatory time. My only hope was to push for the lowest possible sentence. We didn't try the case; we negotiated a plea. But we could not agree on a sentence. I argued for less than ten years. The federal judge gave him sixteen. I was deflated. After winning his acquittal on double murder charges, I still lost him to sixteen years on a drug case where no one was hurt. The irony was brutal: freedom in a case that took lives, prison in a case about money and drugs. These are the breaks criminal defense lawyers face. Sometimes fairness never shows up.

At some point in a law firm, an attorney becomes what they call an "old associate." Senior, experienced, but not accepted into the partner class. The message is clear: make partner or move on. At my firm, I told myself partnership was the goal, mostly because that was the lore. Associates whispered about it, measured themselves by it. Looking back, it was never a serious ambition for me.

Because partnership is not just about whether they choose you. It's also about whether you want to be partners with them. That's the question most associates never ask themselves. There is no room for that question. For many, it's a vacant aspiration tied to money more than meaning. When I asked myself if I wanted to join the ten or so lawyers who ran that firm, the answer was really "no."

There were many reasons, but the biggest was the constant, nagging pressure to prove myself. To jump through hoops, to show I could bring in business and bill like a "money-producing partner." For me, as the only Black lawyer in the firm, that pressure felt like a never-ending test. Could I match the white associates who were being considered? Did I even fit in this world, despite seven years of success there?

Impostor syndrome is real, and it doesn't stop. No matter what I did—win cases, juggle both civil and criminal litigation, socialize, even originate business—my potential felt unseen. I decided I was done being judged in that way. I wanted to work for myself, to practice law at the highest level without politics, without hoops, without anyone else's image of who I should be. I just wanted to do justice.

Leaving felt like the end of an era. I was sad, excited, scared, and happy all at once. On my last day, I walked out of the Federal Reserve Building into unusually warm Boston winds. They blew through my suit jacket as I looked down Atlantic Avenue and wondered what came next. The cobblestones carried me to my car. It felt good. I walked away, and I kept walking.

When I left the firm, I didn't expect my very first case to be a quadruple murder. But that's what landed on my desk, and it would test every skill I had as a lawyer. I built a team that included a private investigator, Flynn, a Harvard student, and a couple of assistants. We met every week, poring over police reports, autopsy photos, and witness statements. The photos haunted me—four young men laid out cold and lifeless, bullet holes marking the end of their stories. I memorized every detail, and they've stayed with me ever since.

My client was accused of murdering four of his close friends in a makeshift basement studio of a home belonging to the parents of one of the victims. It was an old, well-to-do neighborhood in Dorchester, Massachusetts, just two blocks from the Dorchester Division of the Boston Municipal Court—where I would later sit as a judge. From the outside, it was a grand colonial on a corner lot with a front and back yard. The kind of house where you'd never imagine such horror. By the time I saw it, the house had been sold, but I knew it well. I lived in Dorchester then too, less than two miles away, and I drove past it every time I went to court.

The murders shook the city. People didn't want to admit it, but part of the reason it hit Boston so hard was because the young men were not gang members, not drug dealers, not stick-up kids. It should not have mattered, but it did. Their deaths carried a weight that the city had numbed itself to after thousands of shootings.

The basement itself was small, cramped, cluttered, and filthy. To the 19- to 21-year-old aspiring hip-hop artists who spent their nights down there, it was a perfect hangout. Mom and Dad upstairs let their son and his friends be. That night, the 4 young men were shot and killed there at close range. The gun was a   .9 mm that allegedly belonged to one of their crew.

Both my client and another young man were charged. The other defendant pled guilty to being an accessory and gave a version of events that painted my client as the shooter of all four boys. The Boston newspapers covered his plea and sentencing:

The defendant said he regrets not stepping in and stopping the killings, and he expressed hope that relatives of the slain men would consider him someone who made a mistake, "not an animal with no heart." Relatives did not speak with reporters after the sentencing.

The defendant faced 48 years in state prison if given the maximum, but a Superior Court judge sentenced him to 13, citing his remorse, his minimal record, and the lack of evidence he knew his friend would kill. With two years already served, he was eligible for parole in about nine. He refused to testify against my client, who denied being the shooter. "Absolutely not," I said to the press at the time. "We are looking forward to showing that at trial."

The case centered on that basement. I went down there myself more than once, thinking maybe the walls would whisper something the reports had missed. It was dirty and smelled of liquor, smoke, and sweat. I half-expected ghosts to brush past me, but all I found was the stale odor of a place where life had been stolen. That basement, those autopsy photos, and the weight of it all followed me into court every single day.

The trial took place in 2008 and quickly became a media circus. Reporters covered every hearing, and cameras flashed each time I leaned over to whisper to my client. The Boston press reported on every court date and interrupted lawyers to ask for their comments. The courtroom was packed—four families filling the benches, police officers lining the back, and the press jammed into the jury box taking notes. Some days it felt like the whole city of Boston was watching.

As you can imagine, the tension was constant. I had never tried a case with this much publicity. Some people stood so close to the bar that separates the lawyers from the audience I could feel their breath as the handcuffs were put on. Family members of the victims stood inches away from me during recess, close enough to whisper threats as court officers shackled my client. One man leaned in, low enough so the judge could not hear, and said, "You're going to burn in hell."

My client was brought from Nashua Street Jail each day. In lockup, his father gave him court clothes, and four officers walked him into the courtroom shackled at the hands and feet, chained like an old chain gang prisoner. The only thing he carried was a Bible.

I understood the grief of all parties involved, but Suffolk Superior left me vulnerable too. Everyone walked through the same front doors— lawyers, defendants, families, judges, witnesses. That meant I was often in elevators with the victims' relatives or leaving the building alongside them. Sometimes they followed me to my car, standing to watch as I pulled away. It was unsettling.

I lost so much weight during that trial I joked I was back to my fighting weight. The smallest Marines are the meanest, after all. Flynn drove up from Maryland each week to strategize with me. He stayed in Boston through the whole trial, sat in court each day, and was my second seat in everything but name.

Opening statements are always nerve-racking. They are the jury's first impression to decide how they feel about you and your client, long before the evidence comes in. That first morning, the courtroom was packed with press, families, friends, and onlookers, all waiting to hear why a 21-year-old man was accused of murdering four of his friends in a Dorchester basement.

When the judge finally turned to me, my stomach dropped. Sitting at counsel's table, I felt like I would forget my first line, trip on the way to the podium, or throw up in front of everyone. But, just like kindergarten graduation day, I was prepared. I touched my client's shoulder and stood. At first, all I heard was my breathing. Out of the corner of my eye, I saw his Bible on the table. The prosecutor, now a well-formed enemy in the context of this case, sat waiting. Then the words came.

I told the jury who my client was—his life, his family, his aspirations, even his friendship with the boys who died—and why the Commonwealth's version didn't add up. Once I began, my nerves slowly disappeared.

Throughout the trial, even with his life on the line, my client noticed the small things. For instance, he joked about our matching suits, telling me how sharp we looked together. I made sure his family brought him crisp shirts, fresh ties, and well-fitted suits. We both kept clean haircuts. Even facing four life sentences, he had a kind of youthful ease that amazed me.

For me, it was a tightrope. I was Black, young, gay, female. I didn't want to be "too" any of those things in front of a jury. Trials are as much about perception as fact, and I knew they were weighing every detail against my words.

The trial stretched over the summer with more than sixty witnesses. In the end, it came down to deliberations. For a brief moment, I believed we had a chance. There was one juror who refused to convict. But then the trial judge fell ill, the administrative judge stepped in. She questioned her about a past domestic violence case (in which she wa a victim) she had not disclosed on her juror questionnaire and dismissed her. My stomach dropped. The prosecutor smiled.

The next morning, I saw her outside the courthouse. She walked toward me on the ramp and simply said, "Bad news," shaking her head. I knew what she meant.

It didn't take long. Without her, the jury convicted my client of four first-degree murders. Four guilty verdicts, one after another. The air went out of me. My client stood tall, but his freedom vanished with each pronouncement.

My sentencing argument focused on everything else in his life—his family, his support network, his youth, his potential for rehabilitation. It was hard to write because I already knew the outcome. The judge had no discretion on the four murder charges. She was required to impose life without parole. Despite that, I was the only person in that room who could speak on his behalf. I felt like I stood alone between him and every pair of eyes filled with hate.

After closing arguments, then–District Attorney Dan Conley approached me. He said I had done a fine job, that this was what the adversarial process was supposed to look like: two fierce advocates battling it out. I didn't think he even knew who I was before that moment. His words mattered.

Sentencing drew even more people. A courtroom packed with press, victims' families, prosecutors, and what seemed like every police officer in Boston. Photographers lined the jury box, cameras flashing every time I leaned over to whisper to my client. Police officers stood shoulder to shoulder along the walls. I knew the judge had a reputation as a tough sentencer. Again, I would be the only person in the room speaking for him. Such a young life, now destined for confinement.

I thought of a story I once read about a cheetah in South Africa. It chased a dog into a lean-to bathroom. Both animals became trapped inside when the door closed. The cheetah had its prey cornered, yet did nothing. The safari keepers explained that once a wild animal realizes it has lost its freedom, all hunger and desire cease. Depression takes over. I have often wondered if confinement would have that same effect on me. I believe it would.

When I finished my argument, the judge quickly pronounced sentence: four consecutive life terms. I was not surprised, but I was devastated. I told my client some parting words of encouragement and promised an appeal as he was led away. I met with him in lockup, then spoke with his family. That was when a court officer told me the judge wanted to see me in chambers. "Wow, she must really like you," he said. "She never asks to speak to anyone."

Justice Hinkle greeted me warmly, almost incongruously so given she had just condemned my client to die in prison. She praised my trial performance and told me Boston needed more trial lawyers like me. Then she encouraged me to apply to the bench.

She was the second judge to push me in that direction. Years earlier, Judge Edward Redd at the Roxbury Division of the Boston Municipal Court had done the same. But it was on this day, after my greatest courtroom defeat, that I truly considered it. Justice Hinkle did not know it then, but she became the impetus for my first application to the Massachusetts Trial Court in 2009. She later testified on my behalf at my confirmation hearing. Her support of a Black woman doing her best has never been forgotten. She has remained in my corner since the day she sentenced my last criminal client—the one that got away.

During this same period, while running my solo practice, I also returned to the Marine Corps courtroom. Military justice was near to my heart, and now I was on defense.

A Black man raping a white woman. It was a putrid narrative, rotting in my gut. It may date back to Birth of a Nation in popular American consciousness, but the trope began with our arrival on these shores. African slaves were sexualized for breeding, for the captors' pleasure, and as a weapon of control. The irrational fear of a Black man raping a white woman fueled countless lynchings, even as white slave owners completely dominated African bodies. Not even our sex or sexuality was our own. To then reverse that reality and portray African men as sexually dangerous was repulsive beyond words.

I dreaded confronting that lie once more and despised the idea of that centuries-old dynamic obstructing a defensible case. Yet there I was in Japan, representing another Black Marine. This time, a captain. My favorite rank.

A fraternity brother from Omega Psi Phi Fraternity, Inc. introduced him to me, and later I would also represent that brother. I generally liked my clients, and I liked Michael. He was younger than me, with a stellar record of service. Friendly, thoughtful, in phenomenal shape, and a model officer. It was hard to believe he was accused of raping his wife. But he was charged not only with two counts of rape, but also with violating a protective order and several counts of assault and battery.

I flew to Japan three times over 18 months. From Boston to Okinawa is 7,536 miles, a 19-hour trip one way. At the time I was newly in solo practice, so Michael had to cover my travel costs in advance. He did so gladly because he trusted me. Trust is the most important part of the attorney-client relationship, and in military cases, the stakes go far beyond freedom. Pay, pension, health insurance, housing, and a career are on the line.

It felt strange to return to a Marine Corps courtroom not in Charlies and patent leather shoes with red lipstick, but as a civilian defense counsel. For years I had followed the prosecutor's script, the same in every case. But now I was on the outside of the structure I had once belonged to. It felt both odd and affirming. Odd because I was no longer an insider. Affirming because I had done well enough post–Marine Corps to have a client fly me first class across the world to defend him. That felt good.

While there, I stayed in modest hotels, nothing like the penthouse I once rented in Ginowan City overlooking the ocean and American Village. I trained in base gyms, rehearsing my closing arguments as I lifted. A lawyer, like a salesman, must always be closing.

The courtroom was intimidating, especially for the accused. His wife stood firm on the witness stand, her story consistent and difficult to hear. As a woman, her testimony struck me, but as a lawyer, I had to defend Michael zealously. That meant challenging her credibility and suggesting other motives. It required a delicate balance: I wanted the jury to see me as both human and female, but also as a fierce advocate for the accused.

The added layer of race was daunting. For all his rank and record, it still came down to the old cliché: a Black man accused of raping a white woman. The stereotype threatened to undo us. I had to go all out: put Michael on the stand, highlight his service and character, and pursue every weakness in his wife's account and background. It was dirty work, but necessary. There was no time to buckle under the weight.

The charges were among the most serious a servicemember can face, carrying double-digit sentences and career ruin. And throughout the trial, there was an undercurrent of racial animus. Perhaps today, after George Floyd, more people would recognize it. But in 2005, most Americans were unwilling to see the difference in how allegations play out when the defendant is Black and the alleged victim is white.

The Bench
Scars of Justice

Me, Governor Deval Patrick of
Massachusetts, 2013

Judge Frison, Middlesex Superior
Court, 2022

Chapter Eleven

The Appointment

In 2009, I was still a true believer. I believed in justice, truth, and merit. I believed that if you had the skills and the drive, you could achieve anything in the United States. So when I applied to the Massachusetts bench, I did so with the conviction that my record at trial, my knowledge of the court system, my years practicing law, and my service as a Marine officer demonstrated the leadership and ability required for the job. At 39, I was not thinking about politics, quotas, or strategy. I was simply applying for a position I knew I was qualified to hold. Even though most applicants were older, more seasoned, and often wealthier, I fully expected to be chosen because I was the best for the role.

I also carried into that process the weight of what I had already seen in courtrooms: how race and bias shaped prosecutions, trials, and outcomes. In cases like Michael's in Okinawa, I challenged findings, pressed on the subtleties of bias, and tried to make race part of the discourse, even when no one wanted to hear it. At the time, it was not fashionable to raise those issues. In fact, one might say it was shunned. Yet those experiences gave me perspective and sharpened my conviction that justice required more than simply applying the law—it required the courage to acknowledge the role bias plays in its application.

The application process was arduous, tedious, and deeply intrusive. But everyone applying to a Massachusetts court must go through it. It required exhaustive detail: the cases I had handled, the lawyers and judges I had worked with, outcomes, and my entire legal record. Beyond that, it demanded personal disclosures such as spousal information, credit history, judgments, or anything that "might embarrass the governor." Fortunately, I had no issues to report.

I spent weeks, maybe months, completing it during downtime from my practice. Eventually, I hand-delivered copies for every Governor's Council member to the Judicial Nominating Commission at the Massachusetts State House in the spring of 2009.

For many, this process takes months or even years. Some apply repeatedly before securing an appointment. Others never make it. The competition is steep, with many fine lawyers in Massachusetts. But I stood out. I was a Marine, and not many veterans pursued this path. I was Black, female, gay, and young. I had followed the rules, courted the councilors who valued that attention, and kept my reputation spotless. By the time of my hearing, it was a lovefest. The appointment was clear, and within just a couple of months I was sworn in to the Boston Municipal Court.

The swearing-in ceremony was unforgettable. Massachusetts honors the tradition with full pomp and circumstance, and my friends, family, colleagues, and members of the bar all gathered to witness the moment. One of my proudest memories is that one of my sergeant instructors from Officer Candidates School attended. She was a Black woman, tough and salty, the kind of Marine I had always aspired to emulate. I had not seen her since those blistering hot nights in Quantico in 1994 when she was dragging us through the mud, literally. We had reconnected years later, and when I invited her, she came all the way to Boston and even stayed at my home. It was an honor most Marines never experience, and it made that day even more special.

Massachusetts Governor Deval Patrick appointed me to the Boston Municipal Court. The

Chief of that court, Justice Charles Johnson, was a Black man whose presence and leadership carried weight. During my swearing-in ceremony, he addressed the audience and stated that only time would determine the value of my service to the Commonwealth.

When I first came onto the bench, I met my Chief Justice, Charles Johnson. If you have not met him, he is brilliant. Back then, he wore long, flowing dreadlocks, which already told me something about his confidence and authenticity. Before my first day, we met privately. He reminded me that, as a judge, I could no longer do some of the things I had done as a lawyer—parties and such. I said, "Yes, I know, I know." But then he gave me the most important advice of my career: I could not model myself after any other judge. I could not do the "Charles Johnson" on the bench or the "Ed Redd" on the bench. I had to do the "Shannon Frison." That guidance was invaluable, and I still carry it with me every day.

We were not close personally, but he was my chief. That is why, when someone whispered lies into his ear about me, he came and told me directly. At the time, I was still serving on the Boston Municipal Court and had just submitted my application for the Superior Court. On the first day of our annual BMC Judicial Conference, he pulled me into a separate room while my colleagues and I gathered for instruction. He told me about two outrageous lies: first, that I was somehow responsible for a bag of cocaine found in the Brighton Division of the BMC; and second, that I was having sex with a male session clerk at Roxbury—in the courthouse, no less. It was laughable. And I did laugh as he recounted these ridiculous slanders. But then he cautioned me to watch my back.

Here's what really happened: in Brighton, a bag of cocaine had allegedly been "found" under the desk blotter in the first justice's lobby. I had covered that court a few days while the regular justice was on vacation—so had several others. With about 20 Boston judges regularly rotating through the BMC's eight divisions, I was often one of the traveling judges. In a given week, I could be in Roxbury, Dorchester, South Boston, East Boston, Charlestown, West Roxbury, Brighton, or Central. Roxbury was my home court, and I spent much of my time there, though Dorchester was the busiest and demanded a lot of my attention as well. Occasionally, though, I covered Brighton. In fact, I had sat there just a few days in the months before the conference. Somehow, someone tried to connect me to that "discovery."

Of course, I was never questioned by Trial Court security or the Boston police—who were supposedly called and took a report—nor was I informed of what became of the so-called investigation. Years later, when another attempt was made to scandalize my name, I learned that no such investigation had ever taken place. The trial court had no reference to the Brighton incident. The Boston police had only a single-page report stating that someone at the courthouse reported a bag of cocaine. There was no investigation, no interviews, no confiscated substance, no tested substance. As strange as it sounds, the entire story appears to have been nothing more than an attempt to smear my reputation.

Surprisingly, not a word of this story or the sex allegation ever reached the governor, the JNC, the JBC, or the Governor's Council. It never surfaced during my candidacy for the bench, likely because both claims were complete fabrications. Still, being outspoken, young, Black, female, and gay did not sit well with many of the old-timers and pearl clutchers in Massachusetts. Yet, I persisted. And I continued to thrive in that environment despite the attacks. I thrived because my focus remained on serving the Commonwealth and the people who came before me in the courtroom, and because I built lasting, trusted relationships with staff and fellow judges.

Lawyers, of all people and all professions, are the best communicators. And communication is what changes the world. Consider the power of speech, the power of the spoken word. It can be powerful in the negative or powerful in the positive. Just a word. From you, from me. Not just the power to complain, protest, or argue, but the power to make things happen. Ashe`. As judges, we know that our words are impactful, powerful, and carry real meaning for the people before us.

That truth has always been personal for me, and it is why the story of Emmett Till has stayed with me all my life. Most Americans know his name. He was a 14-year-old boy from Chicago, my hometown, who went to Money, Mississippi in the summer of 1955, my family's home state. He was accused of grabbing the arm of and whistling at a white woman named Carolyn Bryant inside her family's store. For that alleged act, he was tortured, mutilated, shot, and submerged in a river by Ms. Bryant's husband and two other white men.

I grew up and went to school in Chicago but spent every summer with my grandparents in Mississippi. That is why his story resonates so deeply with me. You have undoubtedly seen the image of Emmett in his casket, bloated and unrecognizable as a boy of fourteen, and the agony and anguish on Mamie Till's face as she looked at her son's body in the medical examiner's office.

That image is seared into our eyes, our minds, and our hearts forever.

Decades later, in 2007, Carolyn Bryant admitted that what she claimed Emmett had done simply did not happen. She had been 21 when she told the lies that led to his murder. Pause for a moment and consider the significance of that admission—and the tragedy it unleashed. For years, many of us wondered how an adolescent gesture toward a white woman could lead to such horrific violence. Now we know it was only words.

In 2023, Carolyn Bryant died of natural causes. Emmett's accuser is gone. What now of the legacy of Emmett Till and Carolyn Bryant? What now? I have always thought she must have been haunted by her treachery, by how she would be remembered. When people are near death, we often want to set things straight. Did she think her admission set the record straight? If so, it was only a gesture—empty, really. The brutality, trauma, death, humiliation, pain, corruption, and racism remain. All of it is bound up in this story.

And it leaves me reflecting on my own legacy. I spent a lot of time considering how I wanted to be seen and remembered on the bench. What type of judge was I? How would I do the "Shannon Frison"? And what would the people I served feel about their time in my courtroom?

Perhaps that is why the Emmett Till story resonates with me on more than a personal or historical level. As a judge, I knew all too well how lies could be weaponized. Just as words cost Emmett his life, they were later used in attempts to smear my own name. The baseless claims that I was tied to drugs in one courthouse or having sex with a clerk in another were never about truth. They were about discrediting me, about silencing a young, Black, female, openly gay judge who refused to shrink herself. Lies may not have destroyed me the way they destroyed Emmett Till, but they were meant to. That is the destructive power of words—and the very reason I remain committed to wielding mine with integrity.

Chapter Twelve

Built Different

I attended an event at Bentley College in Waltham, Massachusetts, called Celebrating Women in the Workplace. It was a veritable "who's who" gathering with CEOs, judges, lawyers, and government officials. Governor Deval Patrick was the keynote speaker. I arrived late and ended up standing next to the Director of the Judicial Nominating Commission in a packed student center. When the program ended, the audience and the panel spent time fellowshipping with one another and with the governor.

At some point, a middle-aged Latina woman approached me and asked, "Aren't you the judge at Dorchester Court?" I said yes but explained that I had been on the Boston Municipal Court—which often placed me in the Dorchester Division—and was now serving on the Superior Court. She acknowledged that she had seen me on the bench in Dorchester. I still could not recall in what capacity we had interacted, but we exchanged a few pleasantries and moved on to speak with others.

Later, as I headed to retrieve my coat and leave, the woman approached me again and asked if we could speak privately. We stepped to the side of the hallway, and she told me that I had made a positive impact on her life. I was intrigued. She explained that her son had once come before me in Dorchester. He had been charged with violating a 209A restraining order by sending his ex-girlfriend a text that said, "Happy Valentine's Day." Although technically that conduct could support a conviction, in this instance it was clearly a minor infraction. She said she was impressed with how I handled his case, which I eventually dismissed, as well as how I managed the rest of the very busy courtroom. She thought I was wise and calm and that I could discern the truly dangerous people in the community from those who had simply made poor decisions.

Her words deeply warmed me. As it turned out, her son was now a student at Bentley College and doing very well.

Throughout my career on the bench, I constantly thought about my role in the criminal justice system. Was I just another link in a chain of racial bias against Black Americans? Another "government gangster," as one of my late friends called me? Or was I a judge who would give people a fair shake and call it as I saw it?

It has always been my belief that if I, as a Black woman, filled a seat of authority and behaved exactly like my white counterparts, then my presence in that role was pointless. So I have always been vocal, an outlier, and a realist. Before it was fashionable, I was talking about race and bias, about the treatment of Black Americans in this country, about our interactions with police departments, and about diversity and inclusion. Before the murder of George Floyd, there was little traction on these issues in the United States. In most workplaces, it was optional to learn about and confront racial bias.

The worst thing you can do to a diversity, equity, or implicit bias training is make it "optional" or "voluntary." That approach fails for two reasons. First, it sends the wrong message about importance. Events that are optional are often treated as personal-interest activities or affinity-group sessions. They are seen as unimportant for the larger workplace and are easily dismissed if interest is lacking. "Optional" also signals that leadership will not be present. If the boss, the chief, or the head of the organization is not in the room, people assume the training does not really matter.

Second, voluntary programming does not capture the people who most need to hear it. The very individuals who opt out are often the ones who need it most.

Think about the types of workplace training that are mandatory—and recurring. Sexual harassment, cybersecurity, ethics, and more. Yet somehow diversity or bias training is not always placed on the same level. In my view, it is just as important, urgent, and necessary.

I believe in an old-school principle the United States Marine Corps taught me: when important information must be shared with all troops, we hold an "all hands on deck" meeting. No one is exempt because everyone needs to hear the message. The state of race relations in this country requires the same approach. It requires all hands, at all times.

I have been the keynote speaker on the topic of implicit bias for MCLE's Practicing with Professionalism course for newly barred lawyers for the last fourteen years. Sometimes it feels as though we are either talking about diversity and inclusion at events like this, where we feel good about ourselves and about each other, or we are talking about unconscious bias and the harms it produces, where we feel bad about ourselves and about each other. Let us instead discuss bias, diversity, inclusion, and history in ways that allow us to feel the full range of emotions as human beings. We can get better at this.

This country is as divided as it can be short of civil war. I ask you today to consider one thing, one starting place: we do not need to compete with one another to be American. There are endless disputes about what it means to be American, how to show it, and who gets to define it. But it is not a competition. To be American is to be imperfect. If you are truly American, you must claim that imperfection, learn from it, and grow through it.

At the very same time that men and women migrated to this land and resisted British laws, policies, and taxes—eventually demanding independence, going to war, and creating a Constitution that still lives and breathes today— those same settlers instituted the slave trade of African bodies throughout the Americas. Alongside the demand for freedom and independence was the creation of a system that stripped Africans of all freedom for centuries to come. We must accept that contradiction. And that contradiction is American.

So no, I cannot compete with anyone to be more American. Whether you stand for the flag or kneel in protest, whether you believe Black lives matter or blue lives matter, whether you shout "me too," burn Nikes, build walls, or tear them down— let us acknowledge our collective imperfection, our true history, and our greatness.

Sometimes in our practice of law, judges seem infallible, or at least think we are. There is strong pressure for lawyers and judges to be perfect. Never make a wrong ruling or decision. Never lose your temper. Always win your case or your motion. But the truth is that it is our imperfections—shaped by our life experiences, our failures, our shortcomings, our humanity—that make us great in law. I think of all the times I felt broken, when I thought I was not worthy of being a Marine or a lawyer. Yet those very times helped shape me into the person I am today.

We know the power of speech, the power of the spoken word. It can wound or it can heal. It can divide or it can unite. A single word can shift a life, a community, or even the course of justice. As judges and lawyers, we must never forget that our words carry real weight and lasting meaning for the people who stand before us.

In 2019, I was quoted on WBZ by journalist Anaridis Rodriguez in a special story about the lack of racial diversity on the bench in the Massachusetts Trial Court. Why did I speak publicly on this topic? Did I think I'd get in trouble for it? Probably. However, I did so in order to express the truth. To say what every member of the public we serve can clearly see when they walk into our courthouses. And beyond that news program, I have been talking about this issue everywhere I speak.

In that special, I was quoted as saying that I am Black, gay, a Marine, and that you cannot replicate that on the bench. Those life experiences inevitably shape my viewpoint and perspective. I speak openly about this because I want to encourage people of color to apply to the bench. Everyone in the Commonwealth can see why diversity on the bench matters. And once appointed, we have to bring our full, authentic selves to the work. Otherwise, diversity is only optics and has no real impact on how the court operates.

A major part of diversity—and inclusion, in particular—is the ability to be authentic. No mask, no shield, no pedestal, no bars. Authenticity matters. It is what leads us to the truth. But authenticity is not always easy. It can be difficult to be authentic and still fit into the workplace, to mesh with colleagues, or to uphold the image of a particular position—like that of judge. Sometimes, you must be willing to disagree with your boss, to hold a minority opinion, or to be seen as somewhat of a rebel. But that difficulty, that friction, is not meant to stop you. Your success depends on your authenticity, because it is part of what you bring to the table.

Throughout my career, I have felt more aligned with the Black bar. At the 2018 annual dinner for the Massachusetts LGBTQ Bar, I discussed intersectionality, the term coined by feminist scholar Kimberlé Crenshaw, and how overlapping systems of discrimination have affected me. I remain intent on being present and active in both communities.

Being true to yourself in the legal profession is essential. There are too many phonies, fakes, and pretenders. The key to being authentic is merit. No one can stop you when you are the best. Gender, orientation, identity—those are secondary to advocacy, work ethic, skill, and talent. I know there are many things people in the Massachusetts bar, among judges, chiefs, and the Trial Court, do not like about me. I was relatively young. I am gay. I have tattoos. I am outspoken on bias and discrimination. I am visible on social media. And I was a judge.

Being a judge allowed me to be part of conversations that might never have happened otherwise. I became a reference point when colleagues wanted to discuss race. One judge once asked me whether the word "Black" should be capitalized when used to denote race. I said I capitalize Black. I do not capitalize white because I modeled my usage after what I had read most of my life. Considering it more deeply, I believe perhaps both should be capitalized, as should Brown when used to denote an ethnic group. These are false constructs to categorize people, but constructs we wrestle with.

In my experience, Black is generally capitalized in the United States to denote the African diaspora and to give us a proper name that can be capitalized like Italian or Irish. White, by contrast, is used more to indicate membership in the global minority. My former professor, the late Martin Kilson—the first tenured Black professor at Harvard—taught me how Irish, Italians, Germans, Russians, and other white ethnic groups were once segregated and excluded from jobs like police and fire departments. Today, those groups are all called "white." Meanwhile, descendants of Africans and Caribbeans are simply called "Black." The difference is that most white people can still trace their ethnic origins—German, Italian, Irish—while for me, because of the erasure caused by slavery, I cannot. That is why Black has become a necessary stand-in.

Journalist Alexandria Neason wrote in the *Columbia Journalism Review*: "I view the term Black as both a recognition of an ethnic identity in the States that doesn't rely on hyphenated Americanness (and is more accurate than African American, which suggests recent ties to the continent) and is also transnational and inclusive of our Caribbean [and] Central/South American siblings." To capitalize Black, she argued, is to acknowledge that slavery "deliberately stripped" people of their ethnic and national ties. She continued: "African American is not wrong, and some prefer it, but if we are going to capitalize Asian and South Asian and Indigenous, for example, groups that include myriad ethnic identities united by shared race and geography and, to some degree, culture, then we also have to capitalize Black."

So the question remains: should we also capitalize White? Some argue yes, because whiteness, too, is a shared racial identity with historical weight. Until recently, many white Americans did not view themselves as "raced." Capitalizing White challenges that assumption and unmasks whiteness as a racial identity that has been just as historically significant as Blackness. Personally, I think the meaning of capitalizing White is best answered by white people themselves. If you are of French heritage, do you want to be described as French, White, or white?

After I wrote to my colleagues about the issue of capitalization, many of them reached out to me individually. I was not in the habit of addressing issues with them as a group, but when I did, it was to teach. The next time I spoke to them collectively was also about race, after our Chief described a colleague's ruling on a motion to dismiss as "interesting." The case was Lanier v. Harvard.

In that case, Tamara Lanier sued Harvard University, seeking the return of daguerreotype photographs of her enslaved ancestors, Renty Taylor and his daughter Delia. The images had been commissioned in 1850 by Harvard professor Louis Agassiz, who used them to promote theories of

Black inferiority. Harvard preserved the photos in its archives and, when Lanier asked for them back, refused. She turned to the courts, but the law offered no remedy.

I realized my anger about the case came not as a judge but as a Black person in America. I was not critiquing my colleague's ruling, but the jurisprudence and structures that made the facts possible. It is about our bodies. Our bodies are not ours, and they have never been ours. That includes likenesses, as in the case of Renty and Delia, photographed in bondage to serve racist science. Harvard, my alma mater, has held those images for more than a century. And when a descendant sought their return, she was denied.

The grotesque truth is that there is no common law, statute, or constitutional provision that provides a remedy. That enraged me the same way I felt when I first learned that enslaved people's teeth were pulled from their mouths to be used by white owners, or that men and women were forced to breed like animals to sustain the slave population, or that Black women—including my grandmother—endured forced hysterectomies and sterilizations. It enrages me in the same way I feel when I watch our bodies brutalized by police, or when I consider mass incarceration, harsher bail and sentencing, experimentation, lynching, rape. The list is endless. It is about our bodies.

I hope one day our bodies matter in this country we serve. American law has not fully restored our privacy, dignity, and bodily integrity. We lack the mechanisms to address these harms. It is not fascinating. It is horrific—still. Again, colleagues reached out privately, expressing dismay, sorrow, regret. But they would not discuss it as a group. Judicial fear. I will speak more about that in the next volume.

Another example that came to light more recently is the case of Henrietta Lacks. In 1951, while being treated for cervical cancer at Johns Hopkins, tissue samples were taken from her without her knowledge or consent. Those cells—later called HeLa cells—proved to be unique because they did not die after a few divisions. They became the first immortalized human cell line and are still used in scientific research today, decades after her death. Henrietta Lacks was a 31-year-old African American mother of five. Her body was not respected as her own.

Lacks's case is one of many examples of the lack of informed consent in 20th-century medicine. Communication between tissue donors and doctors was virtually nonexistent. Cells were taken without patient consent, and patients were never told how they would be used. At Johns Hopkins, where Lacks was treated, African American patients could receive free care only in a segregated ward. Those patients often became research subjects without their knowledge.

Chapter Thirteen

Tenuous Grasp of Power

Recently, someone criticized my service in the United States Marine Corps. After watching my TEDx Talk, this person claimed I was "misleading" in how I described answering the MEPS doctor's question, "Have you ever had a problem with homosexuality?" Of course I answered "no" and said so in the talk. I made light of the word play, but I did not disclose whether I was identifying as a lesbian or not at the time. And of course, that should not matter.

What infuriates me about the so-called criticism is that, first, the person did not and would not say it to my face; second, they missed the entire point of the story; and third that even today, someone still felt the need to take a jab at an LGBTQ service member who actually served to protect them along with the rest of this nation. Hate is real, pervasive, and dangerous. I salute all the service members, both past and present, who had to serve under the threat of expulsion and criminal prosecution. For those who still anonymously question my service to this country, there are a few thousand Marines you can ask about.

A few weeks after that, I was called a "fucking lesbian" by a disruptive defendant who disagreed with my decision to keep his trial date as scheduled on one of his three matters before the court. A senior court officer had already warned me that he was prone to yelling out during proceedings, spewing conspiracies, and generally being difficult. The petty part of me wanted to yell back, "Fucking heterosexual!" But of course, I did not. I did not even honor his homophobic outburst with a response. I was already directing the court officers to escort him out of the courtroom because, after several warnings, he continued to interrupt me and to berate the prosecutors and the DA's office. Needless to say, you cannot do any of that when I am on the bench. Even as a "fucking lesbian," it is my courtroom. Period.

In 2023, I was accused of being an "influencer." I am not sure if the person meant worldwide influence, social media influence, or something personal, because they did not say it to me directly. But I must admit, changing the narrative around race and ending bias in this country requires influencing hearts and minds. So yes, I intend to influence people to consider bias and the disparities it creates when they are making decisions. And yes, I intend to influence other judges and decision-makers to end the differential treatment of people of color, particularly in our justice system. If that is somehow a knock on my ability to be a fair and impartial judge, then we disagree about the definition of those terms.

Hell, my granddaddy was an influencer. He and my grandmother took a stand during times when doing so could cost you your job, your safety, or even your life. My granddaddy taught me what integrity is. He influenced his children, his grandchildren, and everyone around him to work hard and to be true to themselves. When he left us to join my grandmother and the angels, I was lost. I was older than when my grandmother died, but it was just as hard. Or hard in a different way.

Chapter Fourteen

Mr. E. L. Frison

I think he recognized me at the very end of my visit with him. He had dementia, and I watched his face move from vacancy to familiarity. I could tell he knew "Jib" was standing there. I so wanted him to recognize me, to know that his oldest granddaughter was with him one more day.

I wished it was one of those days long past when I went with him to pick up wood or haul slop for hogs. Or when we grandchildren did chores for him and he gave us a dollar, then took us to the store for penny candy and sodas. Or when we sat across the road from the house where he kept what was almost an animal farm—small and ragtag though it was. He had hogs, goats, chickens, cows, horses, and just about anything else that could be eaten, sold, or traded. We would sit with him for hours and watch him feed, raise, and slaughter animals to provide for his family—his clan. Twelve children he and my grandmother birthed and raised. Twelve. How do you feed that many mouths every single day for years? As a sharecropper, farmer, wood hauler, and iron scrapper? Granddaddy always said he thanked the Lord for allowing him to take care of his family for so many years.

In Panola County, Mississippi in the 1960s, it was dangerous for Black people who tried to register, vote, or participate fully in this country. Extreme violence and retaliation were common. House burnings, lynchings, and brutality against Black citizens were still widespread. It was then that my grandparents both registered to vote, putting themselves and their twelve children at risk. When their landlord, a German man named Wolf, learned of it, he summarily evicted them from the big house they rented—known locally as the "Wolf House." With only a day's notice, my grandfather had to pack up his entire family and leave. No discussion, no consideration, just put out. Most people today cannot fathom that kind of sacrifice just to exercise the right to vote. But my grandparents knew the risks, accepted them, voted, and kept voting all their lives in Mississippi.

All of my aunts and uncles, and my mother, the oldest of the twelve, picked cotton. My Aunt

Emma told me they worked the fields by hand for three dollars a day. A whole day of picking cotton. When it was done, every child handed their pay to my grandfather, who gave it to my grandmother to keep the household running.

But it was not just about feeding and housing everyone. My grandfather was also a protector. He would not let any man abuse his daughters. Cheating and harsh words might be endured, but if he heard that a boyfriend, husband, or ex had laid a hand on one of his seven daughters, he was grabbing his shotgun and heading out the door. I witnessed it many times. He would wait in the woods, travel to Chicago if he had to, train his shotgun, and do whatever it took to defend his girls.

The sight of my great-aunt Hazel—one of my grandfather's two surviving siblings—comforting my mother at his burial broke my heart. Her care, empathy, and sorrow over a lost brother, and my mother's grief over her father, was almost too much to bear. My mother is a rock, the salt of the earth. She left her job as a longtime dental assistant at the University of Illinois to return to Mississippi and care for her aging parents. She gave up her job, her pension, her life in Chicago. For more than twenty years she stood by my grandfather's side. She cared for my grandmother, too, until her death in 2000. We lost her too soon. The pain was sharp. But my grandfather survived her for another seventeen years. Amazing. He gave us his all. He pushed until the very end. That strength is something I can only hope to emulate. How can we not go on when he showed us how to go on after Grandmomma?

I did not think I would go to the wake. I rarely go to funerals or services. I had only been to one in my life—my grandmother's. But once I arrived in Mississippi, I knew I had to be there. And when I got there, I stayed all eight hours of the viewing. I could not leave him. It did not seem right. Where else would I go? I was in town because our rock, our very foundation, had fallen. Where else could I possibly want to be?

I greeted every man, woman, and child who came to pay their respects. I cried with them all. Black folks, white folks, young and old—so many came to say goodbye to "Mr. Scrap Iron." The respect for this man was tremendous. I cannot describe the feeling. It was my last time alone with him, in that parlor. I wished more than anything he could have said "Hey, Jib" one last time and looked at me with joy, as he always did.

Granddaddy, I know, like you told me on the day of Grandmomma's funeral, "Every day ain't gon be Sunday."

Afterword

Scar tissue is not weakness. It is evidence of survival. It forms when the body repairs itself, and it remains as a record that something was endured. The same is true in life. Scar tissue is what individuals and communities carry forward after injury. It is proof of what happened but also of what remains possible.

What you have read in these pages is my story, but it is not mine alone. The details are specific, but the patterns are familiar to many who move through systems that were never designed with us in mind. To be Black in America, and especially to be a Black woman, is to navigate barriers that begin before you take your first step and persist no matter how far you climb.

The data bears this out. Black women make up only about 2% of all attorneys in the United States. In major law firms, they remain almost absent from leadership, accounting for less than 1% of all partners. Representation in the profession has barely shifted in decades, hovering at around 5% Black lawyers overall, far below our share of the population. In the military, women are about 17% of active-duty personnel, and the officer corps remains overwhelmingly male and non-Black. In both professions, walking into the room often means walking in alone.

These numbers matter because they show that scar tissue is not only personal. It is systemic. It is created by institutions that enforce double standards, apply rules unevenly, and demand that Black women prove themselves again and again no matter their rank, their education, or their achievements. Scar tissue is what develops when talent and discipline are met not with equal opportunity, but with doubt and resistance.

We also know from research what many of us already feel: scar tissue does not stop at the surface. The phenomenon of weathering—the accelerated aging caused by chronic stress and discrimination—is real. Black women who report higher levels of everyday racism show markers of faster biological aging. We are more likely to develop chronic conditions earlier in life and with greater severity. Scar tissue is not only a metaphor. It lives in the body.

So the question becomes: what do we do with it? Scar tissue cannot be erased, but it can be used. It can remind us of what was endured. It can strengthen us in the places that were once most vulnerable. And it can map the changes that must still be made.

For the future, several things are required:

1. Truth and acknowledgment. Scar tissue is testimony. We must name the systems and the attitudes that created these injuries.
2. Structural repair. It is not enough to treat symptoms. We need laws, policies, and institutions that dismantle inequity in health, law, economics, and education.
3. Access that is real. Not token gestures, but meaningful opportunities free of bias and conditionality.
4. Generational investment. Scar tissue heals slowly. It will take more than one lifetime to counterbalance what history has imposed.
5. Narrative agency. We must claim the right to tell our own stories, to define our own scars, and to resist erasure.

The challenge for future generations is not to erase these scars, because that cannot be done. The challenge is to recognize it, to learn from it, and to refuse to let it define the limits of what is possible.

We will take the scars we have inherited. We will carry them. We will remember. And then we will build what healing demands—not in spite of what was done to us, but because we know we deserve something better.